Done and Left Undone
GRACE IN THE MEANTIME OF MINISTRY

SCOTT ANSON BENHASE

Copyright © 2018 by Scott Anson Benhase

All rights reserved. No part of this book may be reproduced, stored in a retrieval system, or transmitted in any form or by any means, electronic or mechanical, including photocopying, recording, or otherwise, without the written permission of the publisher.

Unless otherwise noted, the Scripture quotations contained herein are from the New Revised Standard Version Bible, copyright © 1989 by the Division of Christian Education of the National Council of Churches of Christ in the U.S.A. Used by permission. All rights reserved.

Church Publishing
19 East 34th Street
New York, NY 10016
www.churchpublishing.org

Cover image: David J. Fred / Creative Commons
Cover design by Paul Soupiset
Typeset by Denise Hoff
Library of Congress Cataloging-in-Publication Data

Names: Benhase, Scott Anson, author.
Title: Done and left undone : grace in the meantime of parish ministry / Scott Anson Benhase.
Description: New York : Church Publishing, 2018. | Includes bibliographical references.
Identifiers: LCCN 2017040097 (print) | LCCN 2017049991 (ebook) | ISBN 9780898690637 (ebook) | ISBN 9781640650169 (pbk.)
Subjects: LCSH: Pastoral theology. | Church work. | Benedict, Saint, Abbot of Monte Cassino. Regula.
Classification: LCC BV4011.3 (ebook) | LCC BV4011.3 .B44 2018 (print) | DDC 253--dc23
LC record available at https://lccn.loc.gov/2017040097

Printed in the United States of America

*For my wife, Kelly, the love of my life.
Each day she has shown me grace
for the things I have done and left undone.*

CONTENTS

ACKNOWLEDGMENTS — vii

INTRODUCTION — 1

1. Irresistible Grace, Mostly — 15
2. Ascetical Theology for Parish Leadership — 37
3. The Promise of Stability — 57
4. The Promise of Obedience — 73
5. The Promise of Conversion of Life — 91
6. Ascetical Leadership — 109
7. Ascetical Counsel for Parish Leaders — 133

CONCLUSION — 155
(or, How This Might Make Sense and Work)

ACKNOWLEDGMENTS

This book is a product of thirty-four years of ordained ministry in which so many colleagues, both lay and ordained, collaborated with me. They often endured my wild ideas, hairbrained schemes, and occasional orneriness. Their willingness to stick with me and remain my friends has been a great, enduring gift to me. There are too many to name all of them here, but I want to acknowledge a few.

My colleagues and fellow professed members in the Order of the Ascension have been a source of wisdom and compassion for me during my thirty years as a professed member of the Order. They have challenged me consistently and lovingly to help shape my ministry in the *askeses* that are faithful and life-giving.

I have served alongside some remarkable senior wardens over the years: Gordon Avery, Julian Bivins, John Chatham, Maggi Eskridge, Sue Guptill, Ann Harkness, Betty Jones, Meg McCann, Paula McClain, Wes Newman, and Dave Shumate each in their own way taught me how to lead a congregation effectively. I credit them with all the good work we did together, while crediting myself alone for the mistakes I made. They never could talk me out of making what turned out to be those mistakes, but they always tried.

My three children: John, Charley, and Mary Grace grew up as children of a parish priest. It was not always easy for them growing up as my children. I am so proud of them. They have grown into mature, generous, and full-hearted adults who care deeply about this world that God so loves.

INTRODUCTION

I have been ordained for thirty-four years. I served in parish ministry for twenty-seven years, and for over seven years I have served as a diocesan bishop. If I listed all that I have done and left undone in those years, then there would no room on these pages for anything else. The phrase "done and left undone" comes from the Confession of Sin in the Episcopal Church's Book of Common Prayer 1979:

> Most merciful God,
> we confess that we have sinned against you
> in thought, word, and deed,
> by what we have done,
> and by what we have left undone.[1]

Oh, the things I have done and left undone, for both good and for ill in the last thirty-four years! And that is why I have written this book. I also hope others will learn from the many things I have done and left undone and find new hope in their parish ministry. While leading a parish is no simple task, it can be done faithfully and effectively without losing our passion for the gospel, or our sanity and health in the process.

I hope my own failings, and some of what I have accomplished through God's grace, have given me more than a bit of wisdom and perspective on my life, sinner that I am, and on the life of the Church and her leaders. What I have "done and left undone" has often been deliberate, but just as often my own blind spots prevented me from seeing the consequences of my decisions for the Church. This Church, which I love, is the *Bride of Christ*. I truly believe that. I have a "high" ecclesiology. The Church will not go limping out of human history. Jesus will not turn his back on his own creation.

But I also have "low" anthropology.[2] What I have done and left undone has at times made the Church appear to others more like the Bride of Frankenstein than the Bride of Christ. Nevertheless, I still stubbornly insist that what the ordination collect says about the Church in the Book of Common Prayer is true: it is a "wonderful and sacred mystery."[3]

This perspective of a high ecclesiology and a low anthropology is, I believe, at the heart of the Anglican tradition. It is how I understand and interpret the via media we Anglicans often speak about: bringing the best wisdom from both the Catholic and Reformed traditions. A high ecclesiology means we trust in the tradition we have received and are obedient to "Mother Church," even when we do not always agree with her. The Church's collective wisdom over the years is wiser than any one of us. It is arrogant to think otherwise. And a "low" anthropology suggests we should be very wary of our own judgments and motives as individuals and as a church. Trusting ourselves without first holding ourselves accountable to our tradition and to others in the church is a dangerous delusion. Our human propensity to sin means we will get things wrong more often than we care to admit, and that means grace in all things must be our default position.

All this has led me to the conclusion that the church becomes truthful and vital only as we clergy are honest with ourselves about our own sin while being obedient to the tradition we have received. By doing so, we can seek to lead in ways that are faithful to both the claims of Christ and his Church while also leading in ways that are spiritually and emotionally healthy for ourselves and others.

From my observation and experience, when we are committed to the truth about the world and the truth about ourselves, and are also focused on standing in an emotionally healthy and spiritually mature place, then the church tends to get things right more often than not.

Leadership in the Parish

In real estate, they say the three most important considerations are: "location, location, location." My experience has led me to conclude that in the church the three most important considerations are: "leadership, leadership, leadership." But leadership is a word that means too many things to way too many people. It is a word thrown around a lot these days in the church. It has become a word in search of a definition mainly due to our collective anxiety about the church's future.

When people call out for more and better leadership in the church, however, what they are often asking for is someone to lead them in the direction they want to go. People get classified as good leaders only if they are doing what certain people want them to do. Otherwise, they get labeled as "wrong-headed," "misguided," or—perish the thought—"against the gospel of Christ" (at least as a particular group chooses to understand it).

So, in many ways, "church leadership" is a term in search of a definition. I will give you mine:

> Church leaders are those who stand with the people of God bearing the Great Narrative of Redemption in Jesus Christ. As stewards of this Great Narrative, all that they say and do should proceed from the Divine Truth that in the Cross of Jesus, God has redeemed and reconciled humanity.

This is our primary role as leaders in the church. Everything else must be subordinate to the bearing and stewarding of that Great Narrative of Redemption. When we get sidetracked from that primary role or wander down a rabbit hole of the latest fad in the church that seems enticing at the time, we abdicate our leadership calling in favor of becoming CEOs, community organizers, psychotherapists, political activists, or social activity directors.

But I am getting ahead of myself. Throughout my years of ordained leadership, there has been a growing body of material published and conferences held on how one ought to lead in the church. Interestingly, it has grown in direct proportion to our anxiety over the decline of our membership. It has become a post-Christian cottage industry in the American Church all its own. While they have a few permutations and, on rare occasions, snake oil, these publications and conferences basically fall into three different camps (although there are variations of each).

The first method suggests boldness. Get out in front of the people, stake out the vision, and then charge ahead, trusting that the people will follow. The leader is responsible for creating and shaping the vision. This method requires a visionary leader who is willing to lead the charge ahead of their followers. But, of course, this stance is highly dependent on the charism of the leader. They must have a personality that is capable of charming and convincing people so they will follow. What happens to the vision when the leader leaves or their charism fails?

The second approach recommends leading from behind. Find out where the people are going and then help them get there. Here the leader does not cast the vision, but waits for one to emerge from the people that seems to have the most support behind it. This can be a very empowering way to lead, as it insists that the people own the vision they will pursue together. There is, however, a downside to this approach. It can be like the story of the French revolutionary who while sitting at a café saw a mob rushing by and said: "There go my people. I must find out where they are going so I may lead them." Who determines the truthfulness of the vision?

INTRODUCTION

The third leadership stance proposes that the way to lead is to stand with the people, taking the time to listen to them, while the leader and the people together listen to God. From that listening to one another, a vision emerges. Then and only then does the leader step up to call the people to pursue the vision. This can be very time-consuming. During the process, people may run out of patience or—and this happens quite often—people are not spiritually mature enough to work through such a process toward a consensus vision. How then do parish clergy help raise up a critical mass of mature leaders so they together can cast truthful vision?

Advocates of each of these approaches have their points. And sometimes in the right context and at the opportune time their proposed approaches to leadership match what is needed by the church. Yes, they work sometimes. But not all the time, and not in all situations. Each approach is dependent on so many variables like the parish's history, the current context in which the parish finds itself, and the emotional health and spiritual maturity of the people at the particular time and in that particular place. The possibilities of us getting it wrong are, as the Bible might put it, *legion*, if all we can provide is only one kind of leadership.

That is when we can come to resent the so-called church leadership experts and wonder if we can ever get this right. I have read their books and I have gone to their conferences and I have been told "if you just do things this way" or "if you just follow these ten steps to leadership success" or "work through these eight parts of the change process," then "you will be as successful as me." With the advent of social media, we can now read lists of the "top ten keys to church leadership" on our smartphones. At the end of the book that I read or the conference I attended, most often I have felt like a failure.

To be sure, these authors and conference presenters are trying to be helpful to the church's leaders. They have experienced success and they want to share how they did it. But way too often they are just offering overly simplistic solutions for leadership in the church. They are like the doctor who tells a patient to "take two aspirin and call me in the morning" instead of delving into the patient's medical history, asking them good questions about their life, listening to what they say, and then seeking a deeper diagnosis.

A Benedictine Stance in Parish Ministry

Working with and leading God's people is fraught with all sorts of issues and problems because we are dealing with people like us: sinners who get life wrong—sometimes more than occasionally—people who have histories, relationships, and issues that keep therapists, spiritual directors, and life coaches in business. Leading a parish is an impossible vocation,[4] that is, unless leaders begin from a certain grounding and keep a certain stance in the church (more on that to come).

Early on in my ministry I tried to lead the way authors and conference speakers told me. Believe me, I tried. But I just could not be like those successful leaders. I was not them. I eventually came to the awareness that all was right. I was not them. I did not have their charisms. And guess what? They were not me. They were not gifted with my strengths and weaknesses, and they certainly were not ministering in my particular context.

One conference I attended was led by a British church leadership guru who spoke about how his parish church had grown so much and attracted some of the best and brightest of London all because of his new program, which he was now marketing in the States. His parish church was in a posh part of the city right next to Harrods department store. The next morning of the conference, I found myself sitting across from him at breakfast. I told him my parish church was next to the city's largest homeless shelter and soup kitchen, so we had real trouble attracting a posh crowd. He stared at me for a second, smiled, and then shook his head and left to eat his breakfast elsewhere. And, yes, I made my confession the next week for being a jerk on that occasion. There was no "left undone" that morning. I had just "done" being a self-righteous ass.

INTRODUCTION

I tried all the books and went to all the conferences and nothing seemed to help. I even got a master of science degree with a focus on organizational leadership hoping that would be the ticket to getting things right as a parish priest. While my master's work did help broaden my perspective about how to lead human beings in systems, it did not address the underlying challenge of my leadership role. That is when I turned to an ancient source for some wisdom around how I might lead more faithfully and effectively, while also keeping my spiritual health and emotional sanity. There is an old saying that when one has a hammer in one's hand, then everything looks like a nail. In St. Benedict and his *Regula* (or *Rule*) I found a leader who, while staying grounded in his core baptismal identity and purpose in the world, was also willing to adapt, adjust, and be creative in how he led. In other words, St. Benedict had many tools in his leadership belt, not just a hammer.

His fundamental stance was that of grace: the grace of God poured out for humanity in Jesus Christ. God's grace shaped his baptismal identity and it framed his purpose in the world. Grace is the impossibility that God makes possible. Grace is watching a thousand-pound boulder roll into a raging river and then witnessing that boulder float upstream. Grace is God taking sinners like you and me and, through the atoning work of Jesus on the Cross, making what was unrighteous, righteous. Grace is God's scandalous practice in which God upends human expectations about what is just, right, and fair. It is an outrage to our human sensibilities and to our deeply imbedded internal codes for how we humans should reap our just deserts.

St. Benedict knew that if a leader were to both thrive and survive in the monastery (or anywhere else in the church), then such grace must be incarnated in the way the leader led and in the way people lived and served in the community with one another. Grace, then, becomes the necessary currency by and through which we live and serve with one another. And for us in the church (or in a monastery), it must become the way we discern our parish leadership and how we interact with others.

A good example of this grace-filled leadership is how St. Benedict approached the abbot's relationship with all the other monks. He stated that the abbot, as the monastery leader, should treat all his monks *differently*, which may at times appear to an observer as unfair to one monk or, alternatively, showing favoritism to another. (Ah—such is grace.) As St. Benedict writes: "One he must treat with mild goodness, another with reprimands, yet another with the power of persuasion, and thereby accommodate himself according to everyone's nature and capacity of understanding, and thus adapt himself to the other, that he not hurt the flock entrusted to him."[5]

Notice how St. Benedict presumes the abbot is the one who must adapt in his relationship stance rather than the abbot assuming all those around him must adapt to him. Grace, when it is incarnated and operationalized in leadership, is about our adapting and changing our stance toward others and not expecting them, out of some cosmic or internal barometer, to adapt in how they relate to us. Put differently, grace insists that we must be the "adults in the room," that we not get sucked into the practice of insisting that every person be treated the same way or every issue be faced using the same tactic, strategy, or response. We must always be discerning the deeper action of grace in the church, which God is always bestowing.

Yet so many of us do not understand this. On one end of the continuum, we get caught up (and then bound) by some notion that we must treat everyone equally, which hamstrings any ability we have to be open to the thrust of grace. On the other end, we believe that the way we lead is just the way we lead and people must adjust to our stance and style. I call this the "Popeye Principle." (Popeye popularly said: "I yam what I yam.") It is an insistence that we should not have to adapt our stance and style based on our growing experience in our ministry, or in what we have learned from our own context, which is not a mature understanding of leadership, nor does it match what we know about human behavior in systems or in communities. St. Benedict had it right. We need to take an unwavering stance on grace, but hold a subtler, more fluid stance when it comes to how we respond to the people, things, and circumstances of parish life.

Where I Am Going

If any of what I have written so far rings true for you, or if it just sounds intriguing, then what follows may be for you. Here is what I am up to in the pages that follow.

In chapter one, I will briefly make the case that God's grace in Jesus is the core doctrine of the Christian faith and, thus, must be the grounds and stance for all leaders in the church. In other words, grace must be operationalized first in our practical work, in how we relate to ourselves and then how we relate to others. Then grace must form the core of how we lead the church.

With chapter two, I will contend that an ascetical approach to this grace-filled leadership is the only one that works, while also keeping us from being institutionalized in a straitjacket. The ascetical stance begins with engaging life as it is and not as we so often fantasize it to be. It, therefore, begins with our own experience of human sin and from that it develops practices and habits, the ascetical practices of the church (or *askeses*), that seek to acknowledge truthfully the consequences of the sin all around us while also inviting everyone into a deeper experience of God's grace.

In chapters three, four, and five, I will show how St. Benedict's Promise of Stability, Obedience, and Conversion of Life forms a solid stance as the foundation for parish leadership. I will try there to help us begin to shape our own leadership stance around this threefold promise so that we can learn to lead from our inward identity to our outward *askesis*. In other words, how might we have a congruence between our inner life experience of resting in the mercy of God's grace and how we lead others in the Church?

In chapter six, I will offer examples and images of how this leadership *askesis* works in the lived experience of one who leads in the Church. This cannot just be a theory or a list of technical practices in which we ought to engage. If ascetical leadership grounded in grace is going to be of any real use to us, then it must be grounded in the real world and not only as we hope the world might be. I will also bring in voices from the biological and behavioral sciences and popular culture, because they are a source of wisdom for us as well. They can shape and inform our *askesis*, if we are willing to listen.

In chapter seven, I will offer some counsel on how to apply the *askesis* of the Church—what we know from paying attention to our lives and the insights of the biological and behavioral sciences. This learning can help limit the frequency of our boneheaded moves. (I know of which I speak, because I was most often the bonehead who made those moves.) Richard Rohr calls this "falling into mercy."[6] Unless we can admit our "own phoniness, hypocrisy, and woundedness" and let go of our need to "surround [ourselves] with [our] orthodoxies and [our] certitudes and [our] belief that [we're] the best," then we will never understand the grace of God. The *askesis* of the Church's wisdom helps us to admit our own sin and let go of our stranglehold on doctrinal certitude, so that we may receive the deeper working of God's grace and mercy.

In the last chapter, I will summarize how ascetical grace can and should be the way we lead. It is how I believe we can lead faithfully and effectively without having to follow a program or leadership style that does not fit us. In other words, leading from ascetical grace does not require us to be something we are not (and probably never can be). It invites us rather to a way of being (our stance) and an *askesis* (our practices) that will help us be both faithful and effective in parish leadership.

We too often see faithfulness and effectiveness as being mutually exclusive. As this thinking goes, we can either be faithful to the radical gospel of God's grace in Jesus, which will mean we will not be very effective in parish leadership, or we can be effective, which will then mean we must set aside part of that radical gospel of grace to make sure the trains run on time in the parish and things get accomplished. In other words, we must sacrifice faithfulness for effectiveness. But faithfulness and effectiveness are not mutually exclusive, because I have seen them quite clearly manifested together.

Some Considerations

In this book, I modify the theological foundation of grace with the adjective "ascetical." While in the chapters to follow I will unpack that term more, let me just write here that it basically means "practicing," as in the way a doctor practices medicine or a lawyer practices law. It comes from the Greek word *askesis* (ἄσκησις), which literally means to "practice in order to refine." It was often used in ancient Greece to describe the training athletes endured as preparation for a sporting event. In like manner, there is *askesis* we can do to prepare ourselves for faithful parish ministry. There is *askesis* we can do while leading a parish that can keep us sane and focused. And there is *askesis* we can do to incarnate the grace of Jesus in the parish system.

I make no claims that what follows is a work of scholarship. I have kept endnotes and scholarly references to a minimum. There are scholarly works where one can dig deeper, if that is the reader's desire. Instead I draw from the gospel, my own experience, current research on human behavior, recent examples in public life, and my own love of popular culture—particularly music—and connect them to how we truly experience parish life.

My aim here is to provide us hope that we can survive this "impossible vocation" of parish ministry. That is my hope. I love the colleagues I have had over the years in parish ministry. I love the leaders I now oversee as a bishop. They are some of the best human beings I have ever known. Parish ministry is a hard thing to do well. Like me, they do the occasional stupid thing. Who does not? But their steadfast faithfulness never fails to inspire me.

I have subtitled this book "Grace in the Meantime of Parish Ministry," both as an homage to John Snow's masterful work and to employ a dual (duel?) sense of the word "mean." The first sense is more cosmic. We share and experience grace in the "meantime" of ministry: that time between Jesus's cross, resurrection, and ascension and God's great culmination of human history when "Jesus shall reign where e'er the sun doth his successive journeys run."[7] It is this time, in between, when we exercise our leadership in the church.

In the second sense, I use the phrase in its more earthy meaning. Parish ministry can be a "mean" time. I have seen and experienced it myself. People, who in every other aspect of their lives behave professionally and respectfully, somehow feel they have a license to treat clergy in a rude and ugly way. Most of the time they are not doing it consciously. Yet, they still do it. It may be because they are working out anger issues with God or a member of their family. It may be because they believe we are safe people on which to project such meanness (after all, we are supposed to be "nice" to all people, so we will not retaliate). For whatever reason, clergy can be on the receiving end of some harsh behavior by otherwise reasonably kind people. This is a system-wide mystery in the church. At least, it is to me. Such behavior probably has multiple causations that a conference of psychotherapists could explain, given enough time.

If this introduction has in any way intrigued you, then please read on. If not, put this book on your bookshelf in a semiprominent place. The title alone might impress a visitor who happens to wander into your study. Better yet, give it to someone who might find it helpful. They may not, but who knows?

INTRODUCTION

NOTES

1. The Book of Common Prayer (New York: Church Publishing, 1979), 360. Hereafter referred to as BCP.
2. I find the definitions here for low and high anthropology to be very helpful: http://www.mbird.com/glossary/anthropology/.
3. BCP, 540.
4. One of the few books I have read in the last thirty years that has been actually helpful to me as a parish priest is John Snow's *The Impossible Vocation: Ministry in the Mean Time* (Cambridge, MA: Cowley, 1988). I honor Father Snow's work by riffing on his subtitle with this book's subtitle.
5. *The Rule of St. Benedict* (New York: Vintage Spiritual Classics, 1981), chapter 2.
6. Richard Rohr, "Falling into Mercy," The Center for Action and Contemplation, June 23, 2016, https://cac.org/falling-into-mercy-2016-06-23/.
7. Isaac Watts, "Jesus shall reign where'er the sun," *The Hymnal 1982* (New York: Church Pension Fund, 1985), 544.

1

IRRESISTIBLE GRACE, MOSTLY

Begin with Grace

Grace must be where we begin. Before we delve into *askesis* for leadership, we must have a foundation for such practices. If we are true to what the Church has proclaimed for the last two thousand years, then we can begin nowhere else but grace. God's intervening act in Jesus to redeem humanity on the Cross means that everything else must be seen and understood through that cosmic intervention into human history. And that, of course, means God's intervention of grace must shape how we lead. It makes no sense for us to lead with other stances such as utilitarianism, meritocracy, or social Darwinism that at one time or another seem to be the ruling paradigms in Western culture. If grace is true and it is what God has been up to, and continues to be up to in the world, we cannot proclaim it as the very nature of God and then not practice it in how we lead.

Although I am by no means a Calvinist, I am alert to my own life and to the world around me. Thus, certain aspects of Calvinism's TULIP doctrine[1] make a whole lot of sense to me (especially the Big T: total depravity). I recognize such depraved tendencies in myself and, to be fair and balanced, in others as well. Sin is everywhere and all the time. No part of me and no part of the world goes unaffected by it. As the Office of Morning Prayer in the 1928 Book of Common Prayer states: "There is no health in us."[2]

Well, maybe there is some health. Maybe the prayer overstates the human condition a bit. There is "health" in me. My intentions are good at least 51 percent of the time. I am able to do good. I can be kind, compassionate, and just. But I know that even my best intentions can become an avenue for my sin. Echoing the Prayer of Manasseh, I must conclude: "I have sinned, O Lord, I have sinned, and I know my wickedness only too well."[3] (And I know yours too, by the way!)

Still, I understand the biblical witness to be one of God's irresistible grace, mostly. That does not mean we do not resist it. We do in countless ways, sin being what sin is, but God has the last word on humanity's fate. God does not and will not leave us to our own devices. Grace intercedes in our path to personal and communal destruction and snatches us from the jaws of death. And this not only for the "sweet by and by." There is plenty of living death right now all around us as the people of this world live gracelessly. Grace is for now, and not just when we move into the "larger life" with God. In other words, we live knowing how the drama of the human story ends: with the New Jerusalem of John's Revelation coming to earth. And, as we say in the Lord's Prayer, God's kingdom will come one day to this earth "as it (already) is in heaven." God's grace in Jesus makes this possible. The human family, who has seemingly bought a one-way ticket to death and destruction, gets its destiny rerouted by God's intervention on the Cross. Our human trajectory changes from death to life. This is God's final word to humanity.

God's grace, then, should not be seen as God meeting us anything less than all the way. It is not as if God reaches half of the way to us and then waits patiently for us to come to our senses and then we reach the other half of the way. Our good works, our insight, our cleverness, or even our faith do not make up the other half so we can meet God somewhere in the middle. God through Jesus steps into the cesspool of our lives and brings us out all the way. We do not help one bit.

A favorite icon of mine is one I believe is called the "Harrowing of Hell," where Adam and Eve are emerging from prison-like square boxes (like a jack-in-the-box) as the chains fly off those boxes. They are reaching up with their arms from out of the boxes and God's arms appear in the top half of the icon. In a cursory look at the icon, you might see that these two first humans are holding hands with God. But if you look closer, then you see that God is not giving them the "right hand of fellowship." God has them both by the wrists and is literally yanking them out of their imprisonment in death. Neither Adam and Eve, nor we, meet God even part of the way. Martin Luther, it is said, once responded to a man who was bragging that he had accepted Jesus Christ as his "personal savior." Luther asked him something like this: "If someone came up to you and dropped a bag full of gold coins in your lap, would you then go around bragging about how clever and faithful you were in accepting the gold coins? Of course, you would not."

Grace and Human Choice

A few years ago as I was driving home one late Sunday evening, I saw a church sign that read: "Choosy Moms Choose Jesus." It was dark and late and I was not sure what I had read, so I stopped my car, turned around, and went back to double-check. Yep. My hunch is that the person who came up with that message, however unaware, was using an old marketing strategy: be timely and draw on the comfortably familiar to promote your message. It was, after all, Mother's Day and the message related emotionally to a successful ad campaign for a peanut butter brand a few years back. Those two ingredients made the message work. Except it's horrible theology.

The idea that you or I or anybody else *chooses* Jesus is arrogant and gives us way more credit than we deserve. Such a claim presumes that a person has done her market research. She has tested all the other possible saviors or gods out there, weighed their strengths and weaknesses in providing the value she desired for her and her family, and then she chose Jesus, because, of course, she only wants the very best for herself and her family. Jesus then becomes the choice she makes to maximize her return as the choosy consumer of salvation that she is. Like I said, arrogance.

Jesus says in John 15:16 that we did not choose him, he chose us. It is egotistical for us to conclude anything else. As a disciple, I did none of the market research described above. I did not survey the salvation-market landscape and then conclude Jesus was the highest-value alternative among the choices. What actually occurred was quite different. Jesus worked his way past my pride, my self-centeredness, my presumption that I knew best about my life, and met me in the truthfulness of my pathetic, sinful weakness. His grace on the Cross gave me something I had no power to give myself, namely, forgiveness of my sins. I did not choose God's forgiveness. God forgave me in spite of myself.

That church sign manifests a larger cultural distortion of the Christian faith that syncretizes Christianity with modern capitalist presumptions about human behavior. It reflects the *commodification* of Christianity as just another transactional choice we make. But I had no hand in the construction of the Great Narrative of Redemption. Through this narrative, God in Jesus has grasped my life and has compelled me into a drama I had no hand in creating. Any other claim is, as I have said, clearly arrogant. As Lesslie Newbigin has written:

> My commitment to the truth of the gospel is a commitment of faith. If I am further pressed to justify this commitment (as I have often been), my only response has to be personal confession. The story is not my construction. In ways that I cannot fully understand but always through the witness of those who went before me in the company of those called to be witnesses, I have been laid hold of and charged with the responsibility of telling this story. I am only a witness, not the Judge who alone can give the final verdict. But as a witness I am under obligation—the obligation of a debtor to the grace of God in Jesus Christ—to give my witness.[4]

And yet we seem to return constantly to the theme of making the Great Narrative of Redemption to be about our efforts and our accomplishments. As Newbigin contends, we are merely "called to be witnesses" of the story.

Hedging the Great Narrative

A recent survey of Christians who claim they hold orthodox theological views[5] reflects this *commodification*. The survey shows a wide divergence between their views and what the Church has traditionally proclaimed, particularly about God's redemptive grace. Two-thirds of the survey participants responded (and remember, these are self-described orthodox Christians) that we are reconciled with God by our own initiative and then God responds to our initiative with grace. What they are claiming is this: we first seek God out through our own initiative ("Choosy Moms Choose Jesus"), and only then does God respond with mercy and forgiveness through grace. This is how, they say, grace becomes operative in our lives. From my many conversations with Christians across the liberal to conservative spectrum, two-thirds seems about right. It may be even a bit low.

To be fair, this argument has its own internal logic based on Enlightenment constructs of individualism, fairness, and reciprocity (the old quid pro quo, as it were), but it is not the gospel we have received. It nevertheless makes sense to us. It sounds like it should be the way God works, given the intellectual constructs of the Western world. It has a certain "truthiness" to it, as Stephen Colbert might say. Apparently, many of us are so steeped in the deep internal codes of personal responsibility and rugged individualism in Western culture that we like the idea of having a starring role to play in our own drama of redemption. Just one big problem: that has NEVER been the orthodox teaching of the Church.

That brings us to the fifth-century Englishman Pelagius. Yes, he was British, so those of us who are Anglicans must claim him as part of our spiritual family tree. He is like that crazy uncle we have whom no one in the family wants to acknowledge, but own him we must. Pelagius contended that humans first choose God by their own personal gumption. Our sin, original or otherwise, did not, according to Pelagius, impair our ability to choose wisely by choosing God. He thought we must choose to appropriate the benefits of God's grace through the power of our own will. His position came to be known as Pelagianism. Two church councils, first in 418 CE at Carthage and then in Ephesus in 431 CE, rightly rejected Pelagianism. A century or so later, a spinoff of Pelagianism, known rather noncreatively as Semi-Pelagianism, became popular. It sought to affirm the orthodox teaching about humanity's original sin while, at the same time, insisting that humans must take the initiative for God's grace to be operative. In 529 CE, the Council of Orange said, "Nice try, Semi-Pelagianists," and rejected their views.

As I listen to my fellow Christians, it seems to me that the overwhelming majority of us are either de facto Pelagianists at worst, or Semi-Pelagianists at best. God's grace makes us uneasy. Grace does not feel right or fair. It is like we are getting something we do not deserve or did not have to work for at all, that we did not get the old-fashioned way by earning it. It is as if someone gave us something exceptionally amazing at Christmas, something it turns out that we really loved and needed, and it is not that we just forgot to get them anything in return, we actually chose not to get them anything at all. Christmas is the perfect season to illuminate the truth of God's grace. At Christmas, God said, "Here is my baby boy. Do with him as you will." And we did. Oh boy, did we! We laid the wood to him. Then God used our own sinful violence to redeem us.

Self-Justification: No Leg to Stand On

God's grace, and God's grace alone, justifies us before God. We do not even justify ourselves a little bit through own hard work and goodness. A semithorough reading of St. Paul's epistles will result in only one conclusion: we are not capable of justifying ourselves because our sin is a too all-encompassing force over us. As the psalmist says: "Our sins are stronger than we are" (65:3). In fact, St. Paul spends the first four chapters of his Epistle to the Romans making one particular point: "All have sinned and fall short of the glory of God" (Rom. 3:23). He could have saved himself the trouble of writing the first four chapters with just that one sentence.

So, St. Paul, in Romans and throughout his other epistles, urges us to throw up our hands in surrender; to admit that we are no match for sin, and to have faith in Jesus alone to justify us through his sacrifice on the Cross. The only way, St. Paul says, that we "obtained access to this grace" (Rom. 5:2) is through God's justification of us, not through our self-justification. But do we not hear that? It has been, and continues to be, the bedrock teaching of the Church, but so many Christians apparently do not believe it. We spend our lives in an ongoing self-justification project. When we seek to justify ourselves, we trade in the saving gospel of Jesus for a version that says all we really need to do is be a good person. Although we might not admit, it our actions also say we should spend time looking down on others who we think are not as good as we are. We have bought into the idea that the Christian faith is about being good, and if we cannot be good, we can always find others who are not as good as we are. Like the Pharisee who looked down upon the tax collector in Luke 18:9–14 and said (I paraphrase here), "I may be a sinner occasionally. I make no claims to perfection, but look at that guy over there. What a scumbag! Now there's a real sinner." We build ourselves up by tearing others down. Such is the language of self-justification, and we are experts at it.

Our Cultural Formation in Self-Justification

Many of us grew up thinking that church was about being good. I know I did. The church I grew up in was a place for nice girls and boys who obeyed the rules and always had good manners. It was about having pure and clean thoughts, even as we fought off the ones that were not. It was wholesome and sanitary, full of good deeds that proved we were saved, where good boys and good girls drank their milk and cleaned their plates. In high school, the guys in my youth group said, "I won't smoke, drink, or chew, or go with girls who do." Of course, there was more to it than that. The church of my youth also told me that Jesus loved me and saved me. But the church, as I experienced it, said that what really mattered was that I was a good boy, that I behaved myself. Sin was talked about a lot, but only as a cudgel to scare us back into good behavior. I did not begin to understand what grace truly was until I was well into adulthood (and *after* graduating from seminary).

Growing up, I was all about being good and having a good testimony, but deep down inside, I knew that I was not good much of the time. It was a short step for me to conclude that Jesus loved me only when I was good. The catch was this: if I were just good enough, then Jesus would love me. The church's message started out as the gracious word that Jesus loved me, but it wound up in a very different place. It became an ominous threat. Yes, Jesus loved me, but that love seemed to come with certain conditions in the fine print of the contract. Just how good did I have to be and how often? Fifty-one percent of the time? Seventy-five percent of the time? Ninety percent of the time? All the time? I never knew exactly where the goal line was. It kept moving.

If we look at recent studies, many young adults feel betrayed by the church because the church they hear does not sound much like the Jesus they hear in the gospel.[6] What they hear is a church lecturing them about being good but what they see is a church that seems more concerned with obeying its rules and surviving as an institution. And the church bears most of the blame because we have not told folks the truth. We were wrong about who we were and what we were about. Christianity is not about being good; it is not about hanging up our clothes or having good manners; and, I discovered, Jesus does not care one bit whether I clean my plate.

Christianity is not about our being good. It is actually about our regular failure to be good. It is about the brokenness of human life. It is about our repeated inability to be the people God created us to be. It is about how everything about us—even our best intentions and motives—can become an avenue for self-justifying sin. Christianity is not about us being good. It is about God's goodness. It is about what God has done on the Cross of Jesus Christ. In spite of our sin and failures, God has justified us through the blood of Jesus. Our self-justification must stop.[7]

You and I are no better than anyone else in God's eyes. We are no better than the homeless person we meet on the street. We are no better than the drunk we see stumbling into an AA meeting. As long as we pretend we are, we stay trapped in the self-justification business, and that will not save us. Only Jesus and his Cross has the power to justify sinners like you and me. It is time to throw up our hands and surrender. It is time to stop believing we are in some card game with God where we play our ace of good deeds, our king of generosity, and our queen of being a nice person. We need to throw in our cards and admit we are not playing with a full deck. Only God's amazing and forgiving grace justifies us. That is why St. Paul insisted that we "preach only Christ and him crucified" (1 Cor. 2:2). Anything else places us back on the slippery slope toward self-justification. It is so easy for us to go there.

A Hopeful Universalist

Since God's grace is more powerful than even the worst of human sin, I am a hopeful universalist, but I cannot go all the way to universalism without the modifier "hopeful." I am a universalist in that I hope when all is said and done at the end of human history, everyone will accept the gift of God's graceful acceptance of us. And yet, I must hold out the possibility that some in the end will not and instead will reject the gift of grace. That is what hell is, and that is who is in hell. Hell is the place for those who reject the gift of grace. That is what C. S. Lewis claimed in his book *The Great Divorce*. All those who took the daily bus ride from hell to heaven had to do was humbly accept God's gift of grace and heaven awaited them. Lewis makes it clear, however, that some may decide to get back on the bus and return to hell (there is one vignette in the book that has a bishop get back on the bus because he simply could not admit to one of his former vicars that he might well have been wrong about some theological positions he held while alive). Perhaps grace is in some way resistible, but for the life of me I cannot understand why anyone would turn it down.

Bad News before Good News

Grace, God's acceptance of us in spite of very good evidence not to do so, is the primal message of God's Good News in Jesus through his atoning sacrifice on the Cross. It comes to us in the Great Narrative of Redemption in the Bible. But grace, as I have written, has an antecedent: what the Church calls sin. Grace is necessary because of the bad news we have come to know about ourselves. Without sin, there simply would be no need for grace. As Frederick Buechner writes in his book *Telling the Truth: The Gospel as*

Tragedy, Comedy, and Fairy Tale, the good news comes to us first as bad news before it is good news. It is the news that we are sinners; that we are evil in the imagination of our hearts; that when I look in the mirror what I see is at least partly a chicken, a phony, and a slob. That is the tragedy.[8]

Buechner may have made the most honest statement ever about who we are and how we see ourselves when we are all alone staring at our reflection in a mirror, but his statement is insufficient without its conclusion. Buechner continues, "But it [the gospel] is also the news that [we] are loved anyway, cherished, forgiven, bleeding to be sure, but also bled for. That is the comedy."[9]

In the end, it all comes down to God's grace in Jesus. "All other ground is sinking sand," as the old gospel hymn tells us. Or, as my friend Paul Zahl has said, "Grace is love that seeks you out when you have nothing to give in return."

But What about What Jesus Said and Taught?

Up until now, I have not addressed Jesus in the Gospels, only St. Paul in his epistles and, to a lesser extent, the Revelation to John that promises us the hope of the New Jerusalem coming down from heaven at the end of human history. So we ask, "Is grace as central in Jesus's life and teaching as it was for St. Paul?" There have been commentators who contend that St. Paul shaped the Christian narrative in an antinomian way that moved away from the teachings of Jesus and developed a separate religion that did not agree with the Jesus we meet in the Gospels.

Jesus and the Sermon on the Mount

Jesus is God in the flesh. If we want to know the nature of God— what God is like, if you will—then we look to Jesus. We should see in Jesus the grace of God embodied, not only in his atoning work on the Cross, but also in what he taught. In reading the Gospels, we find this congruence of grace in Jesus.

The longest and most comprehensive teaching of Jesus is found in the Sermon on the Mount. In Matthew 5–7, Jesus first lays out God's nature by letting us know who God chooses to bless, in the so-called Beatitudes. If we can know who and what God finds worthy of blessing, then we have an insight into God's nature, because presumably God would not bless that which was not congruent with God's very nature. In the Beatitudes (Matt. 5:1–12), we learn that God blesses the poor in spirit, those who mourn, the meek, those who hunger and thirst for righteousness, the merciful, the pure in heart, the peacemakers, those who are persecuted for righteousness' sake, and those who suffer evil for attending to their discipleship in Jesus. Jesus concludes the Beatitudes by saying that his disciples should "rejoice and be glad" when such evil comes because the Hebrew prophets of old got the same treatment.

Since God chooses to bless the attributes of God's nature, then God is one who has poverty of spirit; who is mournful, meek, pure-hearted, righteous, merciful, a peacemaker, and willing to suffer evil for the sake of such a nature (sounds like the cross to me). Jesus is saying that if we want to throw our lot in with God and participate in God's very nature, then we need to adopt and inculcate these attitudes in our daily lives. How is that going for you? I get some of those right some of the time. The longer I am at this discipleship thing, I get more of those right more of the time, but at the rate I am going, it would take me a thousand years to get them all right all of the time.

Jesus knew that, I believe, when he spoke those words. He, however, did not take one word of them back. As he said: "Not one iota." The first part of his mission was to let us know who God was and what God was up to in the world, so he did not parse words. He is not going to say: "Just kidding. None of those things matter all that much. Just do your best. Try to be nice when you can. It is okay if you don't." No. The Beatitudes tell us who

God is and who God blesses. It is our responsibility if we cannot live our lives in congruence with what God expects. As Jesus says later in Matthew 5:20, God expects righteousness from us, and that is where the second part of Jesus's mission comes in: making righteous the unrighteous on the Cross. God knows I do not have a thousand years to get it right. Neither do you. In Christ, God exercised a core aspect of God's nature: mercy. God's mercy leads to sinners like you and me being justified through the merits and mediation of Jesus and his Cross.

The Beatitudes are just the overture in Jesus's symphony known as the Sermon on the Mount. He is just getting warmed up. Jesus goes on to say that if we traffic in anger, insult, or slander (5:21–26), then we are mere kindling for hellfire. If we look at another person with lust (5:27–28), then that is just the same as if we committed adultery. If a part of our body leads us to sin (5:29–30), then we just ought to get rid of it and live with that deficiency, since it is better to live that way than for us to keep on sinning with that body part. Divorce (5:31–32)? Forget about it. Adultery again. Swearing oaths is a dead end (5:33–37), as is retaliating against evil (5:38–42).

Jesus ends the first movement of his symphony with a riff on loving one's neighbor and hating one's enemy (5:43–48). Loving our neighbors makes sense because they are probably from our family and tribe. Charity begins at home, after all. And hating enemies makes equal sense because they are opposed to us and out to destroy us, but Jesus says we are to love our enemies just as we love our neighbors. Here we get back to being congruent with God's nature when Jesus says that we love our enemies "so that you may be children of your Father in heaven." Loving our enemies is a way to become part of God's own family. It is a way to participate in God's nature. After all, as St. Paul wrote, "God proves his love for us in that while we still were sinners Christ died for us" (Rom. 5:8). We were God's enemies through our sin, but God loved us anyway. It is God's nature to do so.

As this symphonic movement comes to an end, and since we are already not feeling inadequate enough, Jesus, because he wants to leave no doubt where he is coming from, says, "Be perfect, therefore, as your heavenly Father is perfect." So, I ask you, how is that whole perfection thing working out for you? I have read and reread Matthew 5 and it never fails to raise feelings of inadequacy and failure in me. Jesus is not backing down on the expectations for his disciples. "Be perfect," he says and he means it. Yet, the message of the Cross of Jesus is that inadequate failures like you and me are made adequate and given rest and reprieve from their failures. In Matthew 11:28–30, Jesus makes this clear.

> Come to me, all you that are weary and are carrying heavy burdens, and I will give you rest. Take my yoke upon you, and learn from me; for I am gentle and humble in heart, and you will find rest for your souls. For my yoke is easy, and my burden is light.

Jesus is about giving us rest for our souls. We are weary from the heavy burden of trying to be perfect. The yoke of grace actually liberates us if we learn from it. The heavy burden we bear becomes light as Jesus transfers it from our back to his on the Cross.

The Parables of Jesus[10]

If Jesus is consistent, and I believe he is entirely so, then the grace we see in the Sermon on the Mount and his other teachings will also be present in the primary way he communicated, in parables. He told stories to illustrate God's nature and will for humanity to his listeners. Let us look at a few.

The Gracious Father

This parable, more commonly known as the parable of the prodigal son, is very well-known and often misunderstood. We know it has been misunderstood because of the common title it has been given over the years. Why is it named after the younger son in the story? He is but a supporting actor in the drama. It is the gracious father whose actions take the story to its surprising, outrageous conclusion. The story Jesus tells goes (only something) like this.

The younger of two sons decides he has had enough of family life living under his father's rules, so he demands his cut of the inheritance. His father gives it and the young man takes off to the equivalent of Pinocchio's Pleasure Island, where he engages in all manner of self excess. When his money runs out, he is in a pickle. He had not planned for the future. Left with nothing, he gets the only job he can find: slopping the pigs, an awful job for a good Jewish boy. While he is knee-deep in pig slop, he comes to the obvious revelation that he would be better off back home as one of his father's hired hands rather than as he is right now there in the pig slop.

He sets off for home hoping his father will not gloat too much over him and say, "I told you so." He hopes even more that his older brother will just leave him alone and not rub it in. While he is still far off from the old homestead, his father, who has stood on the veranda with high-powered binoculars combing the horizon every day since his son left, spies him limping home. The father drops the binoculars and races toward his son. He moves pretty well for an old guy. When he gets to his boy, he stops. He wants to give the boy some space, given what the kid has been through. The son falls on his knees blubbering about how stupid he was for doing what he did, and how sorry he is now. The father really does not pay any attention to what the boy is saying. It does not matter. All that matters is that he is home. He does not make the kid grovel or trek the rest of the way to the house on his knees. He takes his son in his arms (he's also strong for an old guy) and cradles him as he did when he was a baby. Then he rushes with his boy back to the house yelling like a crazy man, "Get the best clothes out of the closet for him. Find the shiniest bling for his finger. Oh, yes, and get the fattest of the fat calves ready for a barbecue. For this son of mine was as good as dead, but he is back in my arms now. He was lost out there in the world, but now he is back home where he belongs." The parable continues with the second half that deals with the older brother's incredulity at his father's behavior, but I want to stay with the first half of the parable.

All the parables of Jesus give the reader a glimpse into God's nature. In a sense, Jesus's parables answer basic questions, such as What is God like? or What does God expect from us? God, of course, is the gracious father in the parable. God is the one who is scouring the countryside with his binoculars looking for us. When God finds us, God does not wait for us to come begging on our knees. No. God runs to us, embraces us, and carries us back home. This is unmerited grace. Conventional wisdom would be that the father would require the younger son to do some sort of penance, some act over time that showed he had learned his lesson and earned a spot back at the ranch. If not, how would the boy ever learn any personal responsibility? The world's wisdom would say, "Inflict some tough love on the boy. That way he will learn his lesson and never do something stupid like that again." Jesus does not offer tough love. The love Jesus offers is the one-way variety. Is it any wonder that many people do not want to see the deeper meaning in this parable? It upends their understanding of fair play and just deserts. I know it upends mine. God's nature depicted in this parable is outrageous. No self-respecting father would ever do that. Yet, for Jesus, it is exactly what God does.

The Great Banquet

This parable, like the gracious father, has an authority figure, this time a man who has planned for a huge party with a long guest list. The story goes (only something) like this.

When the day of the great party arrives, the day the man has been planning for months on end, none of the invited guests show up. The man guesses that in everyone's busy lives they just forgot about his big shindig, so he sends out word by his servants, reminding those he invited that the day and time have come, so come on down. But when his servants return from the in-person invites, all the man hears are the excuses the invited guests gave for not showing up. One had to wash her hair. Another had to mow his lawn. Still another did not want to miss his favorite TV show. The man, clearly hurt and perplexed by their responses, changes the guest list and instructs his servants to invite the bums on Skid Row and the guys holding signs that read "will work for food." He says, "Go to the charity hospital and get all the wheelchairs they have and roll those folk in here for the party." His servants do so and the banquet hall starts to fill up.

But his servants tell him it still is not full. That would not do for the man. He wanted no empty seats, so he instructs them to go outside his mansion and invite anyone they find passing by to come on in and join the party. In fact, he tells them, "Don't take no for an answer. If you have to, pick them up, hog-tie them, do whatever it takes to get them in the door for the party. I want the house full." Then he mumbles underneath his breath, "None of those sorry folk who ignored my invitation will get to enjoy this spread."

Again, if parables tell us God's nature, then this story tells us that God is throwing one amazing party and wants everyone to join it. God takes the initiative and even compels folks off the street to come in and feast. The participants in the feast were not even on the original guest list. They were minding their own business by the side of the road with sign in hand, or waiting patiently in the hospital for some sign they were getting better and could go home. They did not appear deserving of the invitation. Yet they were brought to the party—some, possibly, against their will. And there was no cover charge at the door. This parable tells us that God is the one who will not take no for an answer (unless we insist upon it) for eternity. God does not wait for us to accept. God is preemptive. God stops at nothing to bring us to the great banquet of fellowship around the heavenly throne.

The Lost Sheep and the Lost Coin

In these two parables, Jesus is addressing a diverse crowd, not just his disciples.

Present were not only the Pharisees and the scribes but also the tax collectors and other assorted sinners—the same crew who heard him tell the long parable of the gracious father. His parable of the lost sheep has a bit of twist to it at the beginning because he asks what appears at first to be a rhetorical question. It goes (only something) like this: "Which one of you fine human beings, if you had a hundred sheep and one wandered off, would not leave the ninety-nine all alone to the wolves and go after that one lost sheep?"

You see what he is doing here? My hunch is his listeners would be thinking, "Well, I'd leave that poor wretch of a sheep to his own devices. I can't sacrifice my entire herd just because one ignorant lamb wandered off. What does he take me for, a fool?" Jesus goes on to say that when the shepherd returns with that one lost sheep, his friends and neighbors are going to rejoice with him. Those listening to Jesus probably were thinking, "No, they wouldn't. They'd be saying to themselves, 'Boy, did he get lucky that the rest of the herd was not slaughtered by wolves. What a dunce.'"

This parable shows the scandalous nature of God, who goes against reasonable behavior to seek us out and find us when we are lost, and then brings us home safely even as his friends and neighbors question if he has a lick of sense. The unspoken point of the parable is the outrageous chance God takes in saving the one lost sheep.

The parable of the lost coin also begins with a rhetorical question. It goes (only something) like this: "What woman, who has ten shiny silver coins and loses one, would stop at nothing to find it?" She is in a frenzy. She gets out her flashlight and lashes it to her broom with duct tape. She sweeps the entire house from one side to the next, from top to bottom. She looks under every rug and behind every piece of furniture. Her neighbors pass by and look in the windows, thinking she has lost her mind. Does she keep on looking until she is exhausted and cannot go on? No. Does she look for the lost coin until she becomes self-conscious about the scene she is making? No. She keeps on looking—until she finds it. When she finally comes up for air and emerges from her house to show her friends and neighbors she has found the lost coin, she asks them to celebrate with her. But as his listeners heard this parable, my hunch is many were thinking, "What a crazy person. She just lost a day's wages to find one coin. Not a good cost-benefit analysis there. She'd have been better off to be thankful she still had the nine other silver coins and write the lost one off on her taxes."

God's nature in this parable defies common human sensibility. God is the woman who no matter what will not stop looking for the lost. No amount of exhaustion or potential public ridicule will dissuade God from searching out the lost and finding them. As with the other parables, Jesus depicts a God who does not make sense, if one is making sense by human standards. God is not prudent. God is not concerned with how things look. God does not appear to care about what seems fair. Rather, God is flagrant with grace. God is inexhaustible when it comes to finding sinners and showing mercy. God seemingly has only one desire: to seek out the lost, especially the ones others may see as undeserving, and bring them safely home.

This is irresistible grace, mostly. As I have written, and I hope the reader now understands, grace is both God's *modus operendi* and *telos*, made possible in the life, death, and resurrection of Jesus. Grace is the very nature of God, at least as God is revealed to us in Jesus.

Grace and *Askesis*

Such flagrant and unmerited grace must form the core of how we lead in the Church. For us to lead from that core stance of grace, however, we need insight and help from what we know about human behavior and how people function in systems. While grace is irresistible, mostly, we humans know how to mess things up—even the best of things. We are messes, as my mother was fond of saying. Francis Spufford in his brilliant book *Unapologetic: Why, Despite Everything, Christianity Can Still Make Surprising Emotional Sense*,[11] creates an acronym for this tendency: HPTFTU or the "human propensity to f**k things up." Once he creates that acronym in his book, he no longer uses the word "sin." He just writes HPTFTU. From my experience of life, it is a completely accurate definition of sin. We humans regularly and consistently "f**k things up." Thus, we need some good *askesis* both to empower healthy, faithful leadership and to mitigate against our HPTFTU, which we do through things done and left undone, to be sure. That does not mean we are left without some capacity to be bearers and stewards of God's Great Narrative of Redemption. We have that capacity. I have seen it all around me throughout my life. But we must see things clearly. We have to see ourselves clearly (self-awareness). We need to see others honestly and compassionately for who they are (empathy). We must understand what is happening around us in the system of the church (insight from experience). And we need to learn from our failures so we do not repeat the same ones too often (there are always new opportunities to fail), so we will not lose our nerve. It is so easy to lose our nerve in parish ministry. Since we know that God has not and will never give up on us, we should not give up on ourselves or on this world that God so loves, and the Church God birthed to bear and steward the Great Narrative of Redemption.

On to *askesis* as the way to faithful and healthy church leadership.

NOTES

1. TULIP stands for: Total Depravity, Unconditional Election, Limited Atonement, Irresistible Grace, Perseverance of the Saints. Matthew J. Slick, "The Five Points of Calvinism," Calvinist Corner, accessed May 28, 2016, http://www.calvinistcorner.com/tulip.htm.
2. BCP, 6.
3. BCP, 90.
4. Lesslie Newbigin, *Proper Confidence: Faith, Doubt & Certainty in Christian Discipleship* (Grand Rapids, MI: Eerdmans, 1995), 82.
5. Kevin Emmert, "New Poll Finds Evangelicals Favorite Heresies," *Christianity Today*, October 28, 2014, http://www.christianitytoday.com/ct/2014/october-web-only/new-poll-finds-evangelicals-favorite-heresies.html.
6. David Kinnaman, *You Lost Me: Why Young Christians Are Leaving Church . . . and Rethinking Faith* (Grand Rapids, MI: Baker Books, 2015).
7. I am grateful to the Reverend Will Willimon, who preached a sermon I once heard and in it used some of the images I have appropriated in this section. I do not know if the sermon was ever printed, but its images have stayed with me all these years.
8. Frederick Buechner, *Telling the Truth: The Gospel as Tragedy, Comedy, and Fairy Tale* (New York: Harper & Row, 1977), 7.
9. Ibid.
10. I am indebted to the late, great Robert Farrar Capon, who helped me hear Jesus's parables with fresh ears. I now cannot hear a parable of Jesus without hearing it through Fr. Capon's writing. Readers will no doubt hear some of his voice in the way I address Jesus's parables.
11. Francis Spufford, *Unapologetic: Why, Despite Everything, Christianity Can Still Make Surprising Emotional Sense* (New York: HarperOne, 2012).

2

ASCETICAL THEOLOGY FOR PARISH LEADERSHIP

Introduction

The term "ascetical theology" is used regularly as a general subset of Christian theology. It is meant to assist Christians toward what has been historically known as "Christian perfection" (which is a dead end, as I wrote in the previous chapter). Here I will use it in its broadest sense, which I believe is faithful to its original use, but not as narrow as what many people may be used to.

The word "ascetical" comes to us by way of the Greek word *askesis* (ἄσκησις). It literally means "to practice in order to refine."[1] The ancient Greeks used the term most often in relationship to athletes training for a sporting goal. *Askesis* was their training regimen so that, when the contest came, they were poised to give their best. That is how I want it to apply to parish leadership and ask, "What are the various *askeses* we need to know how to do if we are going to be faithful and effective in leading God's people?"

A Brief Overview

In the Christian tradition, ascetical theology covers a vast swath of centuries and people, but it is probably first and best known in the Desert Fathers, those intrepid souls who abandoned the first signs of Christendom under the Emperor Constantine in hopes of finding a more profound Christian purity in the desert. In a sense, they went into the desert to go into training. There in the wilderness,[2] a place of danger and deprivation, they hoped they would deepen their faith. Later, ascetical theology was apparent in the rise of various monastic movements where people gathered together to practice a common *Regula*, or "Rule," to more faithfully live out the gospel together. Over the centuries, it has been more closely associated with the Catholic tradition in Anglicanism and has been displayed in the daily practices of Christian life through such sources as the Book of Common Prayer. Ascetical theology is basically applied practical theology, taking the resources and experienced wisdom of the Christian tradition and using them to live more faithfully one's discipleship.

Martin Thornton, an English priest who lived in the mid-twentieth century, wrote extensively about ascetical theology and described it this way:

> I have said that ascetical theology is primarily a practical and synthetic approach to all other branches of theology, and only in a secondary sense is it a "subject" within theology.[3]

Thornton's work was an effort to assist leaders in applying the Church's theology in a practical way to people's lives. In other words, Thornton saw the ascetical theologian's task as synthesizing the Church's theology into a set of practices gleaned from the Anglican tradition for ongoing discipleship. He saw the teaching of these practices as the primary task for parish leaders. According to Thornton, we equip people with the Church's practices (*askeses*) and that deepens their apostolic faith and witness. He wanted people to get out of their heads, so to speak, and apply the wisdom of the Church's time-tested *askeses* for living under God's gracious rule.

Ascetical theology, I think, has been broadly misunderstood as a way to what has been called "Christian perfection." It is commonly mistrusted by those in the Reformed tradition as "works righteousness" under a different name. But as I understand and use it, ascetical theology is as Thornton contends: applying the Church's theology to our life experience and helping leaders live out our identity, purpose, and destiny in a way that is both true to the work of Christ and sense-making for our daily lives. And any sense-making needs to accept the reality of our daily sin and failure.

Ascetical theology does us no good if it does not help us make sense of our lives as they truly are. Its fruit should make our lives more coherent, manageable, and truthful. It should account for what we can reasonably expect from ourselves, given the demands of our lives as they are. It should help us see clearly that we sin seven times before breakfast every morning and given that, how then we might practice our identity and purpose in the world. Ascetical theology helps us fashion a life that is truthful for ourselves and others while resting in the hope of God's grace.

Beginning with the Human Experience of Sin

Any theological approach that does not begin with and take into consideration our real human experience, especially the depths of our sinfulness, will not help us make sense of our experience and the approach will not work for us. That is why the best of ascetical theology begins with the human nature of sin and then addresses our real human experience with the daily *askesis* that nurtures our relationship with God and our neighbors.

St. Benedict, in his Rule, sought practical ways to mitigate the consequences of the many ways we do harm to ourselves and to our neighbors through our HPTFTU (Spufford's "human propensity to f**k things up"). So, let's look at some (and only some) of the recurring sins that all humans experience regularly, how they are manifested in examples from popular culture and politics, and then apply the grace of the gospel to help us get a handle on how to lead a parish where such sin is present in our own lives and in the lives of our parishioners.

Lust

Why not begin here? Lust seems to be everywhere these days. My hunch is there has never been a time when it was not the fascination of the masses. We are sexual beings. The urge of our sexual desire is strong and mysterious. It leads to a lot of other sins we commit in our lives.

Lust is not love. Lust is love reduced to our urges, which means it is not the opposite of love. It is the cheapening of love, or the "disordering" of love, as Bill Stafford has written.[4] It may look like love. Was it love that "launched a thousand ships," or was it mere lust? Either way, any effort at *askesis* of the Christian faith needs to account for it and understand its effect on humans.

Former senator John Edwards, when he was running for president a few years ago, saw his candidacy end when his lust was exposed. He was accused of breaking the law by allegedly using campaign funds as hush money to silence his mistress with whom he had fathered a child. What added insult was his wife's battling cancer at that time (and it would eventually end her life). I am not interested in the politics of the time, or even in the question of whether he broke the law. I am fascinated by his behavior and the choices he made. What was he thinking? He was running for the highest office in the land. While his wife was battling cancer, he had a sexual affair with another woman and fathered a child with her? Lust is a powerful driver in the human psyche. Edwards is not alone as a public figure in doing such things. What was Newt Gingrich thinking when he led the impeachment of then president Clinton (for lying about his adultery) while Gingrich was having an adulterous affair himself? This happens so regularly we are hardly shocked anymore.

Lust leads us to subordinate our lifelong commitments to the utility of satisfying our present desire of the self. This desire to satisfy the self, of course, is not limited to physical desires (what the Greeks called *eros*), but it sure does suck in a lot of the cultural air. Take our Greek philosophical sensibilities, sprinkle in a heavy dose of the French Enlightenment, and—voilà—we have our current *McGnostic* culture, the fast food–like mass marketing that separates what goes on in our heads from what we do with our bodies. We can have all sorts of high and noble thoughts in our heads (both Edwards and Gingrich had them) while using our bodies like amusement parks.

No one with an ounce of Christian sense could conclude that lust is anything less than destructive to the image of God found in every human being, and the destruction is far more than the misuse of sex. That is merely a presenting symptom of the larger disease of our rebellion against God, which many in our culture are pursuing with avid enthusiasm, though not always consciously. God's covenantal love (Hebrew = *hesed*, Greek = *agape*) is the metanarrative of the Bible. It is what drives the Great Narrative of Redemption. God has created us for steadfast love in holy relationships, and not only with God, but with one another in marriage, in friendship, and in our discipleship in Jesus. Our human love and mutual devotion are but a glimpse of the divine love poured out for us in Jesus's life, death, and resurrection.

Love has been on the rap sheet of Christians from the time of Pliny the Younger in the early centuries of the Church to the camp songs of our generation (everybody sing: "They'll know we are Christians by our love, by our love, yes they'll know we are Christians by our love"). But this love is the covenantal love of the Great Narrative of Redemption. It is love that is in it for the long haul with a spouse, a friend, or a fellow disciple. It is love for the other regardless of their utility to us in the present.

Pride

A few years back, I recall hearing former Alaska governor and vice-presidential candidate Sarah Palin make some ill-considered comments about Paul Revere's famous ride. Later, when a reporter gave her an opportunity to reconsider what she had said, she decided to double down on her comments rather than just admit she had been wrong and correct herself. Around that same time, you may recall that former representative Anthony Weiner from New York did something even more ill-considered (I'll let you Google that for yourself—it would make me blush to write it here). When his actions became public, he also doubled down on his lie and claimed his Twitter account had been hacked. He did later confess his lie—well, he did not actually say "lie." We hope for too much sometimes. The lives of Palin and Weiner are just two more reality shows on the network of our lives that illuminate the sin of pride for all the world to see. This sin has been with the human family since the beginning. Human nature is no worse now than it has been throughout human history. The difference these days is that the ever-present media get word out about how our pride leads us to ruin. And yet, although we have recurring evidence about what it does, we still double down on pride.

Pride celebrates the self and the self's accomplishments, often over others and their accomplishments. In extreme form, pride places the self above God and what God accomplished in the Great Narrative of Redemption. Even so-called "self-help" can be a form of pride. Books published with the moniker "Christian self-help" are of no help ("Christian" and "self-help" in the same sentence should give us pause). Such books approach a sin like the sin of pride as though we can cure it by faithfully working harder. But there's no self-cure for the sin of pride. Yet, we think we can balance our pride with a healthy dose of modesty, limiting ourselves to a humble satisfaction and only a diffident delight in who we are and what we have done. Such a balancing act ends up being self-delusional. In his poem "Jordan II," George Herbert tries to pen a poem celebrating God, but gives up when he realizes the object of the celebration is himself ("So did I weave myself into the sense"). Even our efforts that seem selfless can end up serving our self-aggrandizement. He writes:

> When first my lines of heav'nly joyes made mention,
> Such was their lustre, they did so excell,
> That I sought out quaint words and trim invention;
> My thoughts began to burnish, sprout, and swell,
> Curling with metaphors a plain intention,
> Decking the sense, as if it were to sell.
>
> Thousands of notions in my brain did runne,
> Off'ring their service, if I were not sped:
> I often blotted what I had begunne;
> This was not quick enough, and that was dead.
> Nothing could seem too rich to clothe the sunne,
> Much lesse those joyes which trample on his head.
>
> As flames do work and winde, when they ascend;
> So did I weave my self into the sense.
> But while I bustled, I might heare a friend
> Whisper, *How wide is all this long pretence!*
> *There is in love a sweetnesse readie penn'd:*
> *Copie out onely that, and save expense.*[5]

As Herbert concludes in "Jordan II," God's love for us is a "sweetnesse readie penn'd." It's the "onely" cure. All else will delude us into believing that we can strike a balance between our pride (say, 49 percent of the time) and humility (say, 51 percent of the time). It is Sisyphean. The rock will always roll back on us. Without *askesis*, pride can produce in us an all-encompassing exhaustion rather than set loose in us the liberation of grace.

Vanity

Vanity is a close cousin to pride with a large dose of narcissism thrown in for good measure. It is having a higher opinion of ourselves than we ought to have (Phil. 2:3). When vanity takes hold of us, our tongues betray our sin. As James writes, "No one can tame the tongue—a restless evil, full of deadly poison" (3:8). He had a very low anthropology exemplified by our inability to keep our words from spewing forth vain "deadly poison." He concludes, "No one can tame the tongue." If we are self-reflective and honest, we must admit we all occasionally fail to tame our tongues. It is not pretty when that happens. When I look back at the times my tongue was "a restless evil," it was usually when I was feeling inadequate compared to the other people around me or in some way excluded by them. In a childish, vain way, I thought I could build myself up by tearing others down. If I could humiliate them with words, then maybe no one would notice my own failings.

Someone like Donald Trump exemplifies vanity. Mr. Trump acts like me when I have behaved selfishly and childishly; he thinks he can build himself up by tearing others down. He tries to humiliate other people with the "restless evil" of his tongue so no one will notice his own inadequacy. He called former Texas governor Rick Perry a "dimwit." He made fun of Carly Fiorina's face. He said Senator and former POW John McCain was no war hero. He implied a reporter, Megyn Kelly, was menstruating because she had asked him a difficult question he did not want to answer. Such is our vanity. When vanity possesses us, our egos need constant stroking, otherwise we might realize we are not better than everyone else. Vanity is not always as obvious as it is with Mr. Trump. Sometimes it exercises a subtler hold on us. Regardless, it is destructive to our lives in Christ.

Envy

There is a fine line between admiration and envy. Envy is admiration gone spiritually toxic, when we no longer appreciate others for their accomplishments or virtues, but rather our admiration devolves into resentment, desperately wanting what the other has. Often this stance has violent results on both interpersonal and communal levels. As the Epistle of James states in chapter 4:

> Those conflicts and disputes among you, where do they come from? Do they not come from your cravings that are at war within you? You want something and do not have it; so you commit murder. And you covet something and cannot obtain it; so you engage in disputes and conflicts. (vv. 1–2)

The late French historian and philosopher René Girard made this observation about our human condition a part of his theory of "mimetic desire."[6] He contended that all our desires are in a way derived from other people by what we see them desiring. This desire produces "mimetic rivalry" when other people have something we now crave (James 4). Girard said that virtually all human conflict originates in mimetic rivalry. Human culture dealt with this rivalry through religious scapegoat sacrifice, which "paid the debt" of the mimetic rivalry and thus ended the escalating violence. Girard went on to argue that in the Bible God denounced mimetic rivalry through the scapegoating of Jesus while still using his sacrifice to forgive and justify us.

If Girard is right, then it should be no surprise to us that marketers of merchandise capitalize on this mimetic desire and the consequent mimetic rivalry. Take, for example, the Birkin bag, a woman's handbag that costs over $10,000. It's a large, boxy, leather purse owned by the likes of the late Elizabeth Taylor and the very much alive Beyoncé. Women apparently go on a waiting list just to get on the waiting list so they can then someday buy a Birkin bag. They are seemingly always out of stock, marketing the bag by playing hard to get. People who sell the bag haze potential purchasers, which then creates in the one being hazed a sense that someday she might be "worthy enough" to own a Birkin bag.[7]

In a way that echoes Girardian theory, a woman who bought a Birkin bag said: "We all want to be part of some club and that's just out of our reach." She first saw a Birkin bag being carried by a woman walking on her block. She waited for over a year until she was finally found "worthy" enough to own one. She admitted she was aware of being emotionally manipulated the whole time, but after finally being able to have one, she declared, "I just feel more confident when walking down the street with my Birkin on my shoulder."[8] While she was not willing to kill to get one, it was the focus of her attention for over a year. This is not gender-based. Men do the same thing. Need I write about big pickup trucks or the latest electronic gadgets?

Girard was on to something. We know what is happening to us—we know we are being manipulated by mimetic desire and mimetic rivalry—and yet we still fall into this devilish trap, do we not? Such is the power the sin of envy holds over us.

Ascetical Theology and the *Via Positiva*

All of us participate in the above sins and vices to one degree or another, and many of these tend to interconnect with one another, but ascetical theology does not only focus on these and other vices; it also helps us through the *via positiva* with the *askesis* that counters those vices. The *askesis* is summed up in St. Paul's listing of the fruit of the Spirit in Galatians 5.

St. Paul first begins by naming what he calls "the desires of the flesh," which produce the vices, some of which I addressed above. He then contrasts them with what is imparted to us through the grace of God, which he calls the fruit of the Spirit (love, joy, peace, patience, kindness, generosity, faithfulness, gentleness, and self-control). Christ's sacrifice "crucifies" our vices and, as we learn the *askesis* of the Spirit of God, we can grow away from conceit and vanity, competition and pride, and envy and lust. Well, not all the way and all the time, but such *askesis* mitigates the damage our sin can have on us and on others. We are not saved by *askesis*. We are saved by the grace of God. But because of grace, God calls us into a new life. *Askesis* helps us order and shape that new life, and, particularly for leaders, deepen those practices that will allow us to lead well.

Askesis in the Daily Spiritual Practice of Leaders

A few years ago, researchers at Stanford investigated how college students multitasked. They assumed they did it much more effectively than older adults.[9] The researchers expected to find highly toned cognitive abilities that allowed effective multitasking. What they found was that the more people multitasked, the worse at it they were. They were worse at identifying relevant information, more distractible, and more disorganized. They even became worse at what multitasking is supposed to help with: switching tasks seamlessly. Multitasking, they concluded, impairs one's ability to think reflectively. Such reflection is about thinking long enough on a topic to weigh several ideas, which cannot be done in thirty-second bytes while also updating a Facebook page, changing the playlist on an iPod, or watching the latest cute cat video on YouTube.

When we learn to lead with ascetical grace, we can mitigate against the spirit of multitasking. Like Martha in Luke 10:41–42a ("Martha, Martha, you are worried and distracted by many things; there is need of only one thing. Mary has chosen the better part."), we can become so distracted by the busyness of leadership that we feel we do not have time to reflect and pray over our vocation. It is not that we do not have the time. Of course we do. It is that we often lack the courage to live into such a direct, prayerful, and reflective relationship with God. In her book *In Your Holy Spirit: Traditional Spiritual Practices in Today's Christian Life*,[10] Michelle Heyne, OA, addresses the five traditional spiritual practices (Weekly Eucharist, Daily Prayer, Reflection, Community, and Service). Her chapter on Reflection is the one I found most valuable because it is the one practice parish leaders often neglect in the multitasked, Blackberried, and instant-messaged culture in which they lead. We should step back, gain perspective, listen to others, and spend time in solitude so we can think reflectively and prayerfully. Such reflective time is a necessary precursor to right actions. To lead well, we must be able to think and see clearly before we can lead and act faithfully. In Mark 8:23–25, we read:

> When [Jesus] laid his hands on [the blind man], he asked him: "Can you see anything?" And the man looked up and said, "I can see people, but they look like trees, walking." Then Jesus laid his hands on his eyes again; and he looked intently and his sight was restored, and he saw everything clearly.

When we do not make the time for solitude so we can think reflectively and prayerfully, we often end up seeing "trees walking" and not the people, things, and circumstances of the parish that truly matter. As with the blind man, we need more time for Jesus to work on us, more time to listen to the Holy Spirit in our daily prayers and in the prayers of our community. Reflection is not a luxury for when time allows. It is a necessity for which we must make time.

Askesis of Embodying Grace

The Bible tells us we are created in God's image, but it also tells us that our sin has tarnished God's image inside us. This messed-up image explains both our longing for peace and our obsession with war, our ability to love and to hate, and our appetite for filet mignon as well as potato chips. We can watch a powerful drama on one TV channel and switch channels to delight in *The Bachelor*, a show with the moral judgment of a dog in heat. The human species has produced both the great Martin Luther King Jr. and the pathetic, twisted Saddam Hussein. Because we are these mixed bags of divine image and fallen sinner, we have trouble grasping and then trusting in a God who loves us without condition. We need then to be reminded daily of God's grace. Parish leaders are no exceptions. We need to incarnate grace in ourselves so that we may help others embody it in their lives.

A few years ago, researchers at the University of Michigan found that when misinformed people were presented with correct information, they rarely changed their minds. On the contrary, they often became even more strongly entrenched in the misinformation and refused to acknowledge the truth. Truth, the researchers found, did not cure misinformation. It often made misinformation stronger. "The general idea is that it's absolutely threatening to admit you're wrong," said Brendan Nyhan, the lead researcher on the study.[11] Not exactly news to sinners.

Telling someone that God loves them is *not* enough. If they are entrenched in their misinformation, even when confronted with the truth of God's love, they will not accept it as true. Some people are so beaten up by religion in general, or by the way in which they were raised, or by their life experience, that the truth of God's love for them is not something they can accept no matter how many times they are told the truth. That is why we need the *askesis* of embodying God's grace in our ministry.

Brian McLaren in his book *The Secret Message of Jesus: Uncovering the Truth That Could Change Everything* tells a story about his pastor friend Tony Campolo who was having coffee in a donut shop late at night. While there, he overheard a prostitute who was taking a break between tricks say that the next day was her birthday and that she had never had a birthday party in her whole life. So, after talking it over with the shop owner, the next night Tony came back with a cake, candles, and decorations, and he and the patrons of the donut shop threw a surprise birthday party for the woman. She was deeply moved by their actions. So were the other people in the donut shop. The shop owner, who hadn't realized Tony was a preacher, asked him what kind of church he came from.

"I belong to a church that throws birthday parties for prostitutes at 3:30 in the morning," Tony told him.

"No you don't. There ain't no church like that," the bystander said. "If there was, I'd join it."[12]

When we lead with the *askesis* of embodying God's grace, the above story will not be novel to the outside observer. It will be what they see in the parish because we are leading from that place of grace. They will see a parish that looks like Jesus, the one who embodied such grace that not even the grave could contain him.

Askesis in Shaping a Parish Culture of Service in the World

> Holiness is the brightness of divine love, and love is never idle; it must accomplish great things. Love must act as light must shine and fire must burn.[13]
>
> —James O. S. Huntington, OHC

Jesus tells his disciples they are salt and light to the world. Those are powerful metaphors. Salt brings out flavor and zest in food, but we do not eat salt by itself. It is used to enhance the food we eat. Likewise, it would be hard for us to imagine pure, unfiltered light. No one in their right mind simply stares into a bright light. Light, however, like salt, enhances and reveals other things. Light reveals beauty and color, but it also reveals those things we may not care to see, such as poverty and decay. Both salt and light exist for other realities. They direct us to other things.

Our task is to shape the parish culture so God's grace is visible in a world where it is not the norm. As salt and light, we enhance and reveal God's grace to the ungrateful and brokenhearted. Such leadership is exhausting. We may feel like Don Quixote tilting at windmills. Being salt and light must be grounded in something deeper and more eternal than simply the desire to be of greater service to humanity. If we want to shape a parish culture that looks outward in service to God's people, we must ground that service in the worship of God. It is not in serving the world that we come to the awareness that we need to worship God. It is really the other way around. Through our worship of God, we are constrained to do no other than humbly serve all those created in the image of that God. Evelyn Underhill wrote:

> One's first duty is adoration, and one's second duty is awe and only one's third duty is service. . . . We observe then that two of the three things for which our souls were made are matters of attitude, of relation: adoration and awe. Unless these two are right, the last of the triad, service, won't be right. Unless the whole of your . . . life is a movement of praise and adoration, unless it is instinct with awe, the work which the life produces won't be much good.[14]

She is correct. Adoration and awe must precede service. But the quote from Father Huntington is also true. Such adoration and awe, such holiness, cannot remain idle: "It must accomplish great things." We have the task to shape parish culture where this proper order is taught, kept, and nurtured.

Askesis for Dealing with Parish Conflict

Often church leaders must exercise leadership when people who are on opposing sides in a conflict both claim they are standing on principle. Our *askesis* in these contexts is crucial. We must call people to three key types of *askesis*. The first is *empathy*, the ability to place ourselves in other people's context and to try to see and feel things from their perspective. If they are standing on principle, then the stakes are raised. Empathy alone does not solve anything, but it does humanize everyone involved and that may create a margin of grace for a way forward. The next *askesis* is *humility*. It reminds us that even when we are standing on principle, none of us is completely pure in our motives or actions. As sinful human beings, we are inherently incapable of such purity. Humility will keep people honest about themselves even as they take a principled stand. The last *askesis* is *perspective*—understanding the larger context, history, and possibilities. It helps those who take a principled stand avoid rushing too quickly into problem-solving or seeking a quick fix to a conflict. We can help lower their own anxiety and invite others into sharing the same stance, even though they might be on an opposing side. None of these three types of *askesis* offers solutions, techniques, or strategies for people to get their way or prevail in a conflict. We can help people see trying to prevail is counterproductive to building a healthy parish life.

Askesis for Parish Leadership

When I was first ordained in 1983, we were still living in Christendom. Christianity was still the dominant cultural ethos, which meant we could build a new parish church, hire a reasonably gifted priest, unlock the doors, and the people would come. Our evangelization strategy was akin to putting an empty fish tank on the beach and then waiting for the fish to jump in. It worked then, but not anymore. The fish are not jumping into the fish tank these days.

Until recently, the Church's de facto, but unstated, theology of ordained ministry had been that of the chaplain, one who would take pastoral care of the people who showed up in the parish on Sundays and weekdays. Clergy were very good at "chaplaining" people on their spiritual journeys and pastoring people during times of joy (baptism and marriage) and hardship (like sickness and death). As a parish priest, I enjoyed that part of my ministry. It was personally rewarding. But the Church needs more now. We need more leaders who are a skilled combination of chaplain and leader, which is not easy news for clergy to hear. Clergy like myself have had rewarding ministries in the chaplain paradigm. When congregations decline, however, we do not need clergy who will chaplain those congregations to their death. That's ecclesiastical hospice care. Some people in declining congregations are clear that is exactly what they want. They have resigned themselves to death, even if takes a while. If the unspoken stance for many congregations is that of the hospice, who would want to join a parish with that sort of ethos? "Come and join us at St. Swithen's. We are slowly dying and we are satisfied!"

This is a hard *askesis* for us. It is probably unrealistic for us to expect that some people in our congregations will get enthusiastic about mission. Those same people, however, still want the Church to be all that it has been for them and they will resist giving things up for anything new to happen. We should chaplain those people while also engaging others who are open to new mission; this is called "parallel development," where we continue to provide chaplaincy care to one group while working with others to engage God's mission. For this to work, we must partner with other parish leaders and be clear in our role. It is a huge challenge, but we can do it if we have this *askesis*.

Askesis and the Benedictine Promise

> For stability means that I must not run away from where my battles are being fought, that I have to stand still where the real issues have to be faced. Obedience compels me to re-enact in my own life that submission of Christ himself, even though it may lead to suffering and to death. And *conversatio*, openness, means that I must be ready to pick myself up, and start all over again in a pattern of growth which will not end until the day of my final dying. And all the time the journey is

based on that Gospel paradox of losing life and finding it.[15]

—Esther deWaal, *Seeking God: The Way of St. Benedict*

"My promise is to seek the presence of Jesus Christ in the people, things, and circumstances of my life through stability, obedience, and conversion of life." This is the promise taken by members of the Order of the Ascension (to which I belong). I have been reflecting on that promise for thirty years. The interplay of stability, obedience, and conversion of life are the essential elements of the promise. One without the others will not hold.

One night a few years ago, I watched the sun set behind the salt marsh outside of Savannah. The next day, a sister of mine in the Order of the Ascension[16] reminded our fellow professed members that the salt marsh itself is an example of the interdependency found in the Benedictine promise. There the tidal waters work with the plants and animal life to mutually serve and support each other. The tidal waters nourish and feed the cordgrass of the marsh as it comes in, and then it transports food and nutrients produced by the salt marsh to the sea as it goes out and feeds the animal life there.

This mutuality is an apt metaphor for the Benedictine promise. Practicing *stability* grounds us where we are and provides a hedge against our human inclination to run away from difficult things. Steeped in the faith and practice of the Church, we can rest in God and have the *stability* needed for perspective and reflection on our lives. But *stability* without *obedience* and *conversion of life* can make us rigid and can lead us to cut off from others and from the breath of the Holy Spirit leading us to a new place. Practicing *conversion of life* gives us a stance in the world where we are open to that new person, or thing, or circumstance where God just might be calling us. This openness allows us to experience conversion—a change of life—from the place where we are to the new place God is pulling us. This openness comes from the daily practice of repentance, but if our lives are one constant conversion experience, a daily change from one thing to the next, then we become spiritual butterflies flitting about. Practicing *stability* helps ensure our groundedness even as we experience *conversion of life*.

Obedience is like the tidal waters. In the constant ebb and flow of *stability* and *conversion of life*, the practice of listening to God's voice in the Scriptures, the Church's tradition, and the good word from another provides us with the spiritual nutrients we need as we seek Jesus in the people, things, and circumstances of our lives. *Obedience*, the discipline of deep listening to God, to others, and to the pulling of our hearts, gives us competence in our faith practice to discern the way forward. But *obedience* alone can make us passive: always listening, but never doing anything about what we've learned through our *obedience*. *Conversion of life* moves us from the places where we're stuck, reminding us that God is leading us to the New Jerusalem. No metaphor is perfect, but this an apt visual, organic metaphor for how *stability, obedience,* and *conversion of life* work in the Benedictine promise.

The threefold Benedictine Promise has informed and shaped both my thinking about parish leadership and the stance I have taken as one who bears the Great Narrative of Redemption, and how I have led in the parish from that thinking and stance. The Benedictine Promise has provided a framework or a lens by which I have been better able to see my role as a leader in the parish system. The Promise has helped me stay grounded (stability) in a way of being while, at the same time, remaining open to God's movement among the people (obedience) and to the new thing God might be doing next (conversion of life). In the next three chapters, I will reflect on each aspect of the Benedictine Promise[17] and give real-world examples of what that has looked like in parishes, both those I have served and those served by others. What I hope you will get from these reflections and examples is some reassurance that such grounding works for us as a sense-making place for us to stand. I also hope you will see that it works as an avenue for healthy congregational development.

NOTES

1. Greg Peters, "Ascetical Theology," in *The Encyclopedia of Christian Civilization*, 2011, http://onlinelibrary.wiley.com/doi/10.1002/9780470670606.wbecc0089/abstract;jsessionid=EE91BAFE4611C2E7FB99A2B2E23F012B.f04t04.
2. The biblical term for "wilderness" did not connote a place like Palm Springs or some national park like Yellowstone. It meant a place of danger and dread.
3. Martin Thornton, *English Spirituality: An Outline of Ascetical Theology According to the English Pastoral Tradition* (Cambridge, MA: Cowley, 1986), 20.
4. I am indebted here to the work of Bill Stafford, my former church history professor. He and his wife, Barbara, bestowed grace upon grace to me as a young, cocksure seminarian. Bill's book, *Disordered Loves: Healing the Seven Deadly Sins* (Cambridge, MA: Cowley Publications, 1994) is still one I return to time and again for wisdom and insight.
5. George Herbert, *The English Poems of George Herbert*, ed. C. A. Patrides (London: J.M. Dent & Sons, 1974; repr., 1991), 116–77 (emphasis in the original).
6. René Girard, *Violence and the Sacred* (Baltimore, MD: Johns Hopkins University Press, 1979).
7. I learned about this through a piece on NPR. See NPR, "With the Birkin Bag, Hermes Plays Hard to Get," December 31, 2015, www.npr.org/2015/12/31/461627675/with-the-birkin-bag-hermes-plays-hard-to-get.
8. Ibid.
9. Adam Gorlick, "Media Multitaskers Pay Mental Price, Stanford Study Shows," Stanford News, August 24, 2009, http://news.stanford.edu/2009/08/24/multitask-research-study-082409/.
10. Michelle Heyne, *In Your Holy Spirit: Traditional Spiritual Practices for Today's Christian Life* (West Chester, PA: Ascension Press, 2011).
11. See Brendan Nyhan, "New Research on the Effects of Positive Misinformation," January 2, 2013, http://www.brendan-nyhan.com/blog/2013/01/new-research-on-the-effects-of-positive-misinformation.html.
12. Brian McLaren, *The Secret Message of Jesus: Uncovering the Truth That Could Change Everything* (Nashville, TN: Thomas Nelson, 2007), 145–46.
13. Quoted in the Rule of the Order of the Ascension, http://static1.1.sqspcdn.com/static/f/1124858/26280250/1433264322093/The+Rule+of+the+Order+of+the+Ascension+as+of+May+2015.pdf?token=2syc7l4RPN0W4ul47hBWovCaDZY%3D.
14. Ibid.
15. Ibid.
16. From a homily given by the Reverend Susan Latimer, OA, Tybee Island, Georgia.
17. For setting the Benedictine Promise as a core framework for parish life, see the Reverend Robert A. Gallagher's *Fill All Things: The Dynamics of Spirituality in the Parish Church* (West Chester, PA: Ascension Press, 2008), 92–98.

3

THE PROMISE OF STABILITY

What is it then to be stable? It seems to me that it may be described in the following terms: You will find stability at the moment when you discover that God is everywhere, that you do not need to see him elsewhere, that he is here, and if you do not find him here it is useless to go and search for him elsewhere because it is not he that is absent from us, it is we who are absent from him.[1]

—Anthony Bloom

John Keble, priest, poet, and a leader of the Oxford Movement in nineteenth-century England, referenced Benedictine stability in what he called "the trivial round, the common task."[2] It is in these things, Keble asserted, where the opportunity exists "to bring us daily nearer God." It is in the daily and weekly "round" of parish life in which we live and move that we can nourish ourselves as well as give spiritual food to other souls. If we are not feeding our own souls, then we can hardly offer food to other souls. That is why the Daily Office has been crucial to my own soul. Hearing daily the witness of scripture and praying the canticles and the prayers of the Church feeds my soul. I know this. I have regularly experienced it for over thirty years, and yet I am the worst at it. On most days, I must force myself to do it. There is always a distraction that presents itself that seems more enticing. That may be a story I am listening to on NPR, or an e-mail in my inbox that I feel I must respond to (it cannot wait), or something funny one of the dogs is doing that morning.

HPTFTU being what HPTFTU is, I am easily distracted. I am like the dog in the animated movie *Up* that is always having his attention drawn away by the potential of a passing squirrel, which is why I need to resist the temptation to turn on the radio, fire up the computer, check my smartphone, or engage with the dogs before I say the prayers of the Church found in the Daily Office. I know what is good for me. I know what feeds me. I know the grounding, insight, and inspiration I receive from the scriptures and prayers of the Church and yet, one small distraction can send me down the proverbial rabbit hole.

What I practice, then, is akin to the promise found in Alcoholics Anonymous: "One day at a time." Just as the recovering alcoholic promises that only for the coming day they will remain sober, I need to say each morning, "Today I am going to pray the office first before I do anything else." I would like to think I would have the personal fortitude for making that promise for a lifetime, but I know myself too well. I do not have that strength of character. I struggle with what we all struggle. Our culture engenders in us an ethos that seeks the nontrivial and the uncommon, that if we were just somewhere else, someone else, or had something more, then we would be closer to God. If we just had this thing or that charism, then life would be better. If our spouses, or friends, or parishioners, or coworkers were just different than they are, maybe a little nicer and more like us, then our lives would work out nicely and be less difficult. This cultural ethos serves as our very own Uncle Screwtape, as C. S. Lewis wrote.[3]

On the morning that I write this, the Old Testament lesson in the Daily Office is from Ecclesiastes 7. The lesson ends with verse 14: "In the day of prosperity be joyful, and in the day of adversity consider; God has made the one as well as the other, so that mortals may not find out anything that will come after them." The verse calls me back to the Promise of Stability. God has made both kinds of days for me. Some days will bring me joy and some days despair born of adversity. Both days come from God. If I come to expect both and have prepared myself to receive either, come what may, then I am more likely to stay grounded and less likely to be tossed to and fro by that which is immediately in front of me in my ministry.

Another source of wisdom that speaks a similar tone comes from singer-songwriter Van Morrison in his song "Days Like This." Like the preacher of Ecclesiastes, "Van the Man" sings of how our days don't always go as we hope. There will be days when nothing falls into place, when people will not understand what we mean, and, occasionally, when we will be betrayed by even those we love. As my old mentor Glenn "Tex" Evans was fond of saying, "Life is like that."[4] Parish ministry will be full of all kinds of days. That is why the Benedictine Promise of Stability is so essential to my understanding of parish leadership: to not get overly swayed by the joy of a moment in parish life and, equally, to not become overcome when adversity visits. Both will come and both must be received and understood by us as the gift they are. Both are signs of God's presence among us and among the people we are called to lead. After all, Jesus says that God "makes his sun rise on the evil and on the good, and sends rain on the righteous and on the unrighteous" (Matt. 5:45). Stability invites us to stay present in the moment, whatever it is, and not run away.

The truth is, we find God's presence more deeply when we make a conscious, intentional decision not to run away from ourselves, those closest to us, and the "givens" of our lives, but to seek God in those places and people. Such is the virtue of stability. Parker J. Palmer writes, "Community is that place where the person you least want to live with always lives. And when that person moves away, someone else arises to take his or her place."[5] Palmer is right. There will always be people in our lives who seem to make it their life's ambition to make our lives difficult and miserable. The sooner we accept that truth, then the sooner we will benefit from the practice of stability.

The *askesis* of stability helps us accept a certain community, friend, place, or time so we can attend to what is before us and open ourselves up to obediently listen to what God is up to in the present. In so doing, we can become "at home" with a person, place, or event, not waiting for someone or something else to make us feel at home. Of course, for us to practice such "at home-ness," we need to be at home with ourselves. This truth was brought home to me in 2003. I was the parish rector of a growing, complex downtown parish. On our block was a soup kitchen that fed hundreds each day and a shelter for homeless persons that safely housed up to 130 people each night. Having a schedule for each day was somewhat of a sick joke. There was always something swirling around. There were fights to break up, morning prayer to be said, Fifth Steps to hear, the parish sick to be visited, Bible studies to lead, staff to oversee, masses to be offered, sermons to prepare, and the like. After one particularly grueling day in March, a day where I got kicked in the groin by a particularly ungrateful recipient of our help at the soup kitchen, I was driving to the YMCA to work off some of the day's stresses and listening to NPR announce that President Bush had decided it was imperative for us to invade Iraq to find those elusive weapons of mass destruction that Saddam Hussein had so cleverly hidden from a decade of close inspection.

As I pulled into the YMCA's parking lot, my cell phone rang. It was a nurse from the emergency room at the university hospital.

One of my colleagues and a seminary classmate was bleeding out in the emergency room from a massive heart attack. He was asking for me and for the last rites of the Church. I swung my car around and raced to the hospital. I gave him the Ministration at the Time of Death and told him I would stay with him no matter what. I would not leave him. When he was wheeled off to the operating room to try to stop his bleeding, I began calling to track down his parents and siblings. Sixteen hours later, they arrived and I was able to tell them he had miraculously survived the surgery, but the doctors were uncertain whether he would survive the next few hours. If he did, then he would likely live. With his parents and siblings present, I dragged myself home, only to find sheriff deputies seeking to break into the house next door. They had received reports from friends of the woman who lived there that she had not been seen or heard from in days. As her neighbor and her friend, they asked me to enter the house after they secured it. We did. We found her body. Suicide was suspected and later confirmed. She was such a lovely person and a talented artist. She had become a friend of ours and of our children, and an even closer friend to my mother-in-law who lived with us. I was emotionally and spiritually depleted, but I was home with my wife and children.

I slept a few hours and then went back to the hospital to see my friend awake and beginning to return to health. I went to the parish as the Marines pressed on to Baghdad. I walked into my parish office and realized I had missed saying the Office that morning. I promptly went and said Evening Prayer alone in the side chapel. I remember the words washing over me as I cried for the sickness and death all around me and across the planet in Iraq. "Mama said there would be days like this." And God said so too.

I have no doubt that my practice of stability, particularly in saying the Daily Office, allowed me to get through that time of adversity without getting too low emotionally and spiritually. In parish ministry, when all hell breaks loose—and it will from time to time—it is the *askesis* that has sustained us that will define how we endure that time. I cannot explain how I managed that week in my life any other way. I got through it only because I had a pattern and stance in my life that put it in perspective. Such a pattern and stance that we develop is what brings us stability from the outpouring of God's grace. Because of how we practice our ministry (pattern) and what we understand our role to be in the parish system (stance), we can thrive during these kinds of days. To be sure, we cannot thrive forever if those are the only kind of days we experience. In my case, a few days later I went to my wardens (elected lay leaders of the parish) and told them I needed a couple of extra days off in the next week. They knew what I had endured and one of them told me that she was about to call me to tell me to take some days off the following week. What a blessing to have lay leadership such as that. Maintaining such a pattern and stance in our *askesis* is crucial to surviving and thriving in parish ministry. Variety, novelty, and surprise in Keble's "daily round" are not at all helpful. They are truly the last things we need. Parish ministry will certainly give us all three of those, but they come from the outside. Inside we must not be distracted from our pattern and stance, so we will have the capacity and space to obediently listen to God, which Jesus says is the one needful thing (Luke 10:42).

My friend, Fr. Ken Leech, loved to tell the story of Fr. Neville, a long-serving chaplain at a theological college in England.[6] Fr. Neville was quite committed to his Rule of Life and the pattern and stance it provided him. His Rule shaped the whole of his life and ministry. He was much loved by the students and faculty for his gentle demeanor and good humor. While they found him to be a bit of an "odd duck," they cherished and valued his witness to them of a life given over to God. Every afternoon, part of Fr. Neville's daily spiritual practice was to take a nap from 2:00 pm to 4:00 pm. Regardless of what was going on in his life, in the life of the college, or in the life of the world, at 2:00 pm he would stop whatever he was doing, retire to his quarters, and take that nap. One morning, the dean of the college received an urgent message that the bishop of the diocese needed to see him that very afternoon. This presented the dean with a dilemma. He was hosting a visiting bishop from Africa and this bishop was scheduled to speak and then lead a symposium for the entire student body and faculty that afternoon. The dean could not stand up the bishop, so he went to Fr. Neville and asked him to host the visiting bishop for the rest of the day, introduce him at the symposium, and close the gathering with prayer. This visiting bishop was scheduled to speak at 2:00 pm. Fr. Neville readily agreed to stand in for the dean. The dean, much relieved, made plans for his trip to the bishop's office. That day after lunch, Fr. Neville met with the visiting bishop, and after a good visit during which they became acquainted, he escorted him to the auditorium for the symposium. Fr. Neville welcomed the students and faculty, gave a warm and thoughtful introduction of the esteemed visiting bishop, and as he came to the podium, Fr. Neville quietly excused himself and went to his quarters to take his nap. He arose, as was his custom, at 4:00 pm and returned to the auditorium just in time for the symposium to conclude. He stepped to the podium, thanked the visiting bishop for an outstanding presentation, and closed the symposium with a prayer.

While I have always found this story hilarious, I have also appreciated what it has taught me about my own spiritual pattern and stance. As Jesus helped Martha see in Luke 10:41–42, we are "worried and distracted by many things; there is need of only one thing." Jesus knows us better than we know ourselves, does he not? Jesus knows how tempted we are to worry and be distracted by so many things. The demands of the parish never stop. There is always one more thing that needs doing, whether it is that person in the nursing home I had been meaning to visit or getting a wrench to stop the toilet in the bathroom from dripping water all over the floor. It does not stop. So, we better. Staying with our pattern and stance helps us stop, go back to what sustains us, and remember our place and role. Yet, we still are tempted to run away from others and ourselves, which means we need to listen with grace to the grumbling of our own hearts so that we can accept responsibility for why we so often seek to blame others for what is happening in our own lives, or for why something in the parish is not going as we had hoped. This is also a nasty "gift" from Uncle Screwtape.

In my early days of ordained ministry, I spent entire sermons blaming others for what I later saw as merely the adjectives that accurately described the worst parts of myself. My friend Don Johnson, Bishop of West Tennessee, once described the most profound prayer not found in the Book of Common Prayer: "Lord, help me accept those parts of myself I call other people."[7] In those sermons I would exhort people to greater faithfulness without asking the same thing of myself. I would tell them to give sacrificially without doing so myself. Oh, the blaming I did about injustice in the world while also believing that such just living was not necessarily a prerequisite for me. If my parishioners would have been more faithful, more generous, and more just, then the parish would have been the perfected body of Christ. In vestry meetings, Bible studies, and committee meetings, I would describe all the insufficiencies I found in our parish life. I would then be shocked by the pattern I created from the stance I took. Of course, if we would all be more faithful, generous, and just, life would be great, but that is not the point. I was creating an unstable system by my constant negativity and dissatisfaction with the way things were. I was leading from an inner life where I was not at all content with myself as a sinner beloved of God, so I certainly had no capacity to engender grace in my outer life of parish leadership.

It was not until I developed the pattern and stance of stability that I began to relax my demanding tone and my repetitive need to point out the deficiencies of what passed for the Christian life in the parish. Once I gave myself a break from needing to be perfect, I could extend the same break to everyone else. Of course, we should strive for the best expression of the Christian faith in our parishes, but if in our striving we become anxious, petty, sarcastic, demanding, and full of blame for everyone but ourselves, then we quite clearly are creating a parish climate that will reflect our own adjectives. The implications are profound. Given enough time and effort, we create, or at least largely contribute to, the adjectives of the congregations we lead. We can shape congregations as places that incarnate adjectives like grounded, prayerful, reflective, intentional, openhearted, and generous. They will become places where God is taken very seriously, but where people can have a lightness about themselves and where humor and fun are welcome. But that only happens when we incarnate such adjectives in ourselves. Over time, those adjectives will be the words that people use to describe the congregation.

We can never "fix" our congregations through our *askesis* of stability. What we can do is work on ourselves. As we inculcate stability in our own lives, we will see it over time become present in others. I have seen this happen even with those who find it difficult to be "at home" with themselves. I have seen anxious, scattered, and insecure people learn to find some sense of being at home with themselves and God through their experience of the congregation's stability.

Sabotaging Stability

In fact, the more stable the parish culture is in its rhythm of Eucharist, Daily Office, and opportunities and space for people to gather to pray and reflect on their lives, the more the parish can welcome and tolerate people on the emotional and spiritual margins without ceding control of the parish to them. In many congregations, especially where there is not enough emotional and spiritual stability emanating from the leadership, people who have personality disorders, unaddressed anger issues, or just a general spiritual immaturity often rule the climate of the congregation. They take emotional hostages or passive-aggressively insist that if they do not get their way, then in some form there will be hell to pay. They will do their best to sabotage the parish's stability because it threatens their own identity. If we allow these people to dominate, we will live in a constant reactive mode to their various outbursts and threats. Most often, these threats are not overt and stated in writing; it is enough that they are implied to force a reaction from us. My experience tells me that much of the time these people do not even know what they are doing. Since they are not emotionally or spiritually stable, the way they behave and the stance they take within the parish are all they know how to do. Their emotional and spiritual instability is normative for them.

These are the kinds of people who will become most reactive when we begin to practice the adjectives of stability in the congregation. Probably unconsciously, they will see stability as a threat to their normative experience. When we begin to offer and encourage participation in the Daily Office, for example, these people may react by saying they would prefer we teach classes on all sorts of prayer from a variety of traditions, even those outside the Christian faith. They may react even more strongly to preaching that is grace-centered, criticizing us for being "soft on sin." Because they are so unaccepting of themselves, they cannot imagine a grace-filled God who is accepting of sinners like them.

My Experience of Attempted Sabotage

I ran head on into such a situation of great reactivity when I entered one parish as rector. The parish was led by some remarkably gifted, focused, and centered lay leaders, and yet, there were a handful of people who were working through their own anxiety, volatility, and insecurity by demanding control of the parish system. During the interim period before I arrived, most of the lay leadership placated them, often in a good way, by making sure their voices were listened to and not marginalized. But sometimes it was not done in a healthy way. They elected a few of them to the vestry and placed others in leadership positions in the parish.

When I arrived, I began to lead in a way the Church prescribed (presiding at vestry meetings, preaching most every Sunday, working to develop the prayer life of the congregation), and a few of these people seemed to go berserk. I was accused of all manner of authoritarianism. I was called a fascist by one of them because I would not invite him to staff meetings (he was not on the staff of the parish). At first, I was taken aback by the reaction I was getting from doing what I was ordained to do. I slowly realized what was going on as I got to know the people and understood the parish culture. The emotionally and spiritually healthy lay leadership helped me to see the situation, encouraged me to hang in there, and said it would get better. "Who knows?" one of them said with a smile. "Maybe they will just leave." It made me wonder what plan he was hatching.

One person in the group that was so reactive to me started a petition to have me removed as rector, which she later sent to the bishop. If I had not been grounded in the Promise of Stability, then running away would have been an attractive option. I continued to lead in the ways I knew were healthy, keeping an open stance and a listening ear, but also exercising my appropriate authority within the system. Within two years, two of the couples that had been the prime drivers of reactivity to my leadership moved to other parishes (one dramatically resigned from the vestry with a long speech at her last vestry meeting accusing me of countless character defects and sins). Maybe it was my perception, but the Sunday after these two households left, there was a noticeable joy and lightness in the air. People were making eye contact with me and smiling. They were laughing and seeming to enjoy being together in the parlor after Mass. I remember thinking it was like being in Oz after Dorothy threw water on the Wicked Witch and she melted, removing the spell on her subjects. Everyone turned to her and said, "Hail, Dorothy." No one was saying "Hail, Scott," but that day began a new pattern we developed with one another. Within a few years, the congregation grew by 50 percent. I am convinced that growth began, not because those two households left, but because a critical mass of leaders insisted they would not give into immature people's behavior. Rather, we stayed focused on what we believed would bring greater health and wholeness to the parish.

Stability Is Not a Quick Fix

The Promise of Stability does not bring a quick fix to any parish. A parish that is grounded in the Eucharist and daily prayer of the Church, one that is clear about its baptismal identity and purpose, and one that remains open to listening to all voices (even those on the spiritual and emotional margins) will over time create stability within its parish culture. That culture, over an even longer period, will shape people in their own faith practice. The Promise of Stability is for the long haul. Stability is inculcated in others as it becomes our *askesis* in the parish.

Over time congregations, or any human system, will take on the adjectives of their leaders. Those adjectives will form the norm of the system, for good or ill. When healthy adjectives describe the system, then faithful stability occurs and the parish can afford to maintain a certain number of people within the parish family who are emotionally on the margins or who are fragile. They will be welcomed and cared for. The parish will generally understand that these people need the stability of the parish culture because they might not make it in the world without such grounding. In such a stable and healthy parish, however, no one would seriously suggest they be nominated for the vestry or be placed in an important leadership position.

A Word to the Wise

Parish life, like the rest of life, is difficult even when we stay focused on our own *askesis* of stability and work to incarnate that in the rhythms of parish life. For years we can work to shape a healthy, vital parish culture and still the possibilities for hurt feelings born of misunderstandings are seemingly without end. Motives can still be questioned. ("I'm sorry, but you must believe me—I really did not intend for the acolytes to eat that much junk food at the Acolyte Festival.") Sermon illustrations can be wildly misunderstood. ("I was not talking about you in that funny story.") A poorly chosen word at the coffee hour can still be painful for those on the receiving end. ("Did I say 'heavy'? I did not mean 'heavy.' I don't know what I meant. Sorry.") Even when we are doing our best to be attentive to what is happening, we can grossly misunderstand what is going on. And, boy, can we be misunderstood.

When I was a missionary in Honduras over thirty years ago, one of my assignments was teaching the Honduran national anthem, "Tu Bandera," to my fifth graders at St John's School, Puerto Cortes. The irony of that has never left this *norte americano*. It is not just that, as anyone in the church can tell you, I have a hard time carrying a tune, but what was I doing, a young man from *los Estados Unidos*, teaching young *hondureños* their own national anthem. My certainty ever since then has been that there are now sixteen or so middle-aged *hondureños* out there who sing their national anthem slightly off-key and with an awful Ohioan-infused Spanish accent.

One incident in my teaching life in Honduras constantly reminds me of how easy it is to be misunderstood even when seeking faithfully to be attentive to others. I had recess duty after the school lunch one day, and a second grader named Castulo ran up and told me, in Spanish, what I translated as, "Rodrigo is swallowing his pencil." I looked over toward Rodrigo. He was bent over at the waist making spitting movements and noises. Since I had trained as an emergency medical technician in college, I knew what I had to do. The situation called for immediate action, not more information. I rushed over to Rodrigo, where his sounds of distress had only increased, and put my training into action. I positioned myself behind him and performed the Heimlich maneuver. I brought my double-fist up under his solar plexus and below his xiphoid process, as I had been taught to do, and jerked my fists violently back through him and toward me, which had the expected result of forcing his lunch up and out onto the playground. I was confident that I had stopped his choking and saved his life. I looked for the leaden culprit among his undigested lunch, but there was no pencil. Students gathered around wide-eyed, asking, "Maestro, qué pasó?" Castulo then repeated what he had said to me and I realized the horrible mistake I had made. The boy had said, "*Se masticó*" (he chewed) rather than "*Se tragó*" (he swallowed). Chewing one's pencil was against school rules. Like a lot of normal boys his age, Castulo only wanted to snitch on Rodrigo. Oops! Word went out. From that point on, students at St. John's School in Puerto Cortes, Honduras, never chewed their pencils again. The punishment for masticating one's pencil was very severe. A burly red-headed teacher would come up behind you and force you to lose your lunch on the playground! I was trying so hard to understand and to be helpful, but I just scared a bunch of children and made things worse.

In our parish ministry, even when our motives are pure—mostly—the wrong things can happen. We should never assume that our Promise of Stability will inoculate us or our congregations from the normal misunderstandings of living with other human beings. We will always have such misunderstandings. They happen among the best of friends, so why should we assume they will not happen in parish life? I know some leaders who develop a list of rules for how the vestry or other committees will act with one another. ("No talking about the meeting later in the parking lot.") I have no problem, per se, with such efforts, provided the people who will be governed by it create the list. If we impose such rules upon a group through our authority, then they may perceive it as an effort to control diverse voices and opinions within the group, which always ends badly.

Some reality here: we cannot control how another person will handle misunderstandings or hurt feelings because of our interaction with them. They may walk away or stay engaged. But we can do our best to control how we behave and the stance we take in the parish. We can refuse to walk away (or run away, because that feeling will come). We can work to stay connected and try to understand the other person or group involved, to remain engaged long enough for God's love and mercy to work their way past our misunderstandings and our more than occasional need to justify ourselves. We can make the long-term relationship more important than whatever satisfaction might be gained from the other person acknowledging that we were right and they were wrong. I know leaders who seem obsessed with parishioners acknowledging that they were right and the parishioners were wrong. When we are grounded in Stability, we will not need to get the last word in or insist that we were right. We can let it go. Stability reminds us that we are in this for the long haul, which is why we must see our role as being vigilant maintainers of Stability in the life of the parish once it is achieved. Remember, Stability is not the status quo—"the way we have always done things around here." It is the constant grounding of oneself and the parish in the Great Narrative of Redemption. The Church is grounded in that Great Narrative as it gathers for the Eucharist each week, keeps the Daily Office, and remains prayerfully open and self-reflective on its common mission to the world outside its doors.

NOTES

1. Quoted in the Rule of the Order of the Ascension, http://static1.1.sqspcdn.com/static/f/1124858/26280250/1433264322093/The+Rule+of+the+Order+of+the+Ascension+as+of+May+2015.pdf?token=2syc7l4RPN0W4ul47hBWovCaDZY%3D.
2. John Keble, "New Every Morning Is the Love," *The Hymnal 1982* (1822; New York: Church Pension Fund, 1985), hymn 10.
3. C. S. Lewis, *The Screwtape Letters,* reprint ed. (New York: HarperOne, 2015).
4. Glenn Evans, *Life Is Like That* (Nashville, TN: Appalachia Service Project, 1990).
5. Parker J. Palmer, *The Company of Strangers: Christians and the Renewal of America's Public Life* (New York: Crossroad, 1983), 120.
6. I do not know if Ken ever wrote this story down in a book or paper. If he did, I do not know where. He told me this story in a personal conversation years ago. Ken refers to the same Fr. Neville in his book *Spirituality and Pastoral Care* (Eugene, OR: Wipf & Stock Pub; repr., 2005), but does not relate this story.
7. Bishop Johnson attributed this as coming originally from Martin Bell, his friend and the author of *The Way of the Wolf* (New York: Ballantine Books; repr. 1983).

4

THE PROMISE OF OBEDIENCE

I shall cleave to thee with all my being, then shall I in nothing have pain and labor and my life shall be a real life, being wholly full of thee.

—Augustine of Hippo[1]

The first degree of humility is obedience without delay. This is the virtue of those who hold nothing dearer to them than Christ; who, because of the holy service they have professed, and the fear of hell, and the glory of life everlasting, as soon as anything has been ordered by the Superior, receive it as a divine command and cannot suffer any delay in executing it.[2]

—The Rule of St. Benedict, chapter 5

Obedience for St. Benedict was quite simple: do what the superior commands "without delay" as if it were a "divine command." We may think such simple obedience was easier for people of St. Benedict's day than it is for us today, that in his time authority was respected much more and people just did what they were told when given a command from a superior. When the abbot said "Jump" everyone asked, "How high?" on the way up. But St. Benedict lived with human beings just like us. That is why he, throughout the Rule, addressed the issue of grumbling about following certain aspects of it. Humans are not easily given to the *askesis* of obedience, now or then.

Our Great Narrative of Redemption begins in a garden with disobedience. God instructs Adam and Eve to eat of the whole garden with one exception—the fruit of the tree in the middle of the garden. The Genesis story does not specify how long it was between that command given by God and the disobedience of Adam and Eve. My hunch is that it was, at best, forty-eight hours. How long was Moses on the mountaintop before the people of Israel were disobedient to God's command, "You shall have no other gods before me"? Did David delay long once he spied Bathsheba? Disobedience is at the heart of the Great Narrative. Our profound, recurring inability to be obedient to God's law necessitated the Incarnation of God in the person of Jesus. Disobedience, it seems, comes natural to us.

St. Benedict knew that if a community gathered around the truth of the Great Narrative of Redemption had any chance at being vital, then members of that community had to learn obedience. But he hardly advocated a blind, arbitrary obedience born of random or capricious orders from a superior. The Great Narrative of Redemption, since it is the free gift of God's grace, called forth, in St. Benedict's mind, a response of obedience from all those who attended themselves to that story, including the abbot. Obedience is expected so that faithfulness might grow as its fruit in the context of community life. One's obedience is to the community's Rule (and, by extension, to the Great Narrative of Redemption) and not to a person in authority. The person in authority, whether the abbot or some other monk, was under the same Rule. All were subject to it so that all might learn faithfulness. It is overly simplistic to classify Benedictine obedience as "just following orders." Obedience is the yoke of grace that Jesus offers and that the member willingly puts on.

While the Rule of St. Benedict seemingly covers every aspect of how its members should be obedient, there is a clear recognition in the Rule for calling the community together to discern on a given weighty matter not clearly stated in the Rule. In chapter 3 of the Rule, St. Benedict says the whole community should be called together to discern what course of action should be taken. St. Benedict insists that everyone should be heard—even the youngest, least experienced monks—"for the Lord often reveals to the younger what is best."[3] After hearing from all, the abbot discerns what action to take, but even this must not be arbitrary. The abbot must decide in a way that reflects the "prudence and justice" of the community. The abbot, after all, is just as subject to the Rule as everyone else. Obedience, therefore, is not just about following orders from a superior or doing what one was told to do in the Rule merely for the sake of compliance. That would make the Rule primarily about following the law. It was and is holy listening. It is coming to the truth that our only way is Christ's way. Christ came not to do his own will, but the will of the One who sent him. As the Promise of Stability grounds us, we then have the space and time to truly live into the Promise of Obedience, which can become fruit as it leads us to holy action. There is no shortcut. Faithful obedience must come before faithful action.

Obedience is grounded in God's word as revealed to us in scripture as we read it with others in community and as it is prayed over by the church. Obedience to the Word of God is obedience to Jesus. It is not obedience to one's own interpretation of the Bible. That is a distorted understanding found in some aspects of Reformation theology that is still very much present in our culture today. This distortion has become secularized in the ethos of hyperindividualism where everyone gets to be their own spiritual tyrant, or at least an expert on what the "plain meaning" of scripture is. Thus, obedience is not an individualistic practice. It can never be if it is faithful. Left to our own devices, we can construct all sorts of rationales and justifications for our actions. We can all live in denial about our obedience and subsequent actions. The practice of obedience liberates us from the shackles of the distorted ethos of hyperindividualism, which, we should know, undermines every level of community in our culture today.

St. Benedict understood how central community was to obedience. It is our communion with one another that creates the context for holy obedience. In communion, listening, and discernment, we seek God's will. In communion, hope, and decision we seek to obey and act. We need an obedience that is not grudgingly given, that does not foster, as St. Benedict wrote, "a grumbling in our hearts," but rather an obedience that intentionally places us vulnerably open to the communion of saints. This is how we bear the seal of he who died.[4]

Obedience in Leaders

We who exercise our leadership in the church are called to incarnate such obedience. We cannot lead well without this practice. This is not an expectation of perfection; it is a hope that others will see in us a clear stance of seeking obedience in our leadership role. St. Benedict did not expect perfection from the abbot. He had a clear-eyed sense of human frailty. What he demanded was that no one be put in a position of leadership who did not first demonstrate a profound work toward obedience in his own life. One cannot ask for obedience as a leader without first exemplifying such obedience in one's own life. When parishioners see in us a willing self-giving to obedience, then they see the invitation to be drawn into the Great Narrative of Redemption. The opposite is also true: when they see us living and leading in such a way that obedience is held loosely or ignored all together, they will probably not be drawn into such self-giving obedience. For us, it is about where our heart is. It is about a transparency in our lives where others can see in us a desire to be obedient, even when we sometimes fail to be so.

My Disobedience

It was a little thing I did. It was part of a long process the parish had entered into to transform and develop our property for a more effective ministry. We began an ambitious capital campaign to change some of our existing space and add on significant space to increase our capacity for mission. We added a large parish hall and kitchen so the existing space could be transformed into a beautiful atrium for the Catechesis of the Good Shepherd. We added a gorgeous outdoor garden with a worship space and columbarium. We built enthusiasm and commitment for this campaign and it was funded with not nearly as much struggle as I had expected. A small part of the overall plan was to paint and fix up the nave, sanctuary, and side chapel. It involved repainting the nave and chancel's interior walls, swapping out the old brass communion rails at the side chapel for newly designed ones that would match the wooden ones at the high altar, and putting down a new carpet runner in the chancel that would run up into the sanctuary. This small part was not as spectacular as the new parish hall and garden so most people did not pay as much attention to it.

During my entire time at that parish, I had been frustrated that the space between the reredos and the altar was so shallow. The presider could not even turn sideways when presiding. They would have to shuffle sideways to move in either direction when behind the altar. We planned to address this by removing one of the risers and bringing the altar forward the length of one step, which would buy us about ten more inches and not change the view congregants had when looking at the altar. They would not even notice it. But that was not enough for me. I wanted another ten inches. I was not willing to go through the process of making that case to the building committee, cochaired by a longtime parishioner who felt he had compromised on the first ten-inch extension. I went to the subcontractor doing the carpentry work right before the carpeting went down and asked him how much effort and cost it would take to bump out the length of one more step. We would still have plenty of room between the altar and communion rail and I would have my ten more inches. He said it was nothing at all and he would have it done that morning.

The next day, which was the day before the carpeting was to be laid, the building committee cochair happened to tour the progress being made and noticed the additional bump out. He was furious. He found me finishing my weekly Bible study and got up in my face. He accused me of all sorts of nefarious sins, and he was right. I took his tongue lashing and was humbled. I told him that, although I still thought bringing the altar out ten more inches was needed and justified, I had gone about it in the wrong way. I told him I was wrong. I told him I was sorry and that what I had done was underhanded and had not shown my best self. I promised him I would change it back to the original design.

It was lunchtime by then and I had no plans other than grabbing a quick bite to eat, so I set aside lunch, went into the sanctuary with the tool box from the trunk of my car, and began ripping out the extension the carpenter had so carefully crafted. About fifteen minutes into my demolishing work, the building committee cochair walked up behind me. He could have stood there gloating in victory, having exposed the rector of the parish in his underhandedness. What he did next amazed me. I looked back to see in his hand his own toolbox. He smiled and simply said: "I'll start on the other side and we'll get this done in no time. Afterward, you can buy me lunch." We both laughed and I did buy his meal.

It was a small act of disobedience—hardly David and Bathsheba worthy—but it could have turned into a big thing. I had violated the trust of those whom I was called to lead. I had worked years at developing that trust in me as their parish priest. That same building committee cochair was the junior warden when I was called to be the rector four years before. He had told me then that the parish had loved their former rector, but they did not always trust him because sometimes he would do things without consulting the vestry or seeking parish consensus. I remember taking his words to heart. Now, I had done the exact same thing. My one small act of disobedience threatened to undo all my hard work. He could have easily spread the word of my misdeed throughout the parish's opinion makers. He did not. Grace intervened out of my humiliation. I would like to think I was practicing Benedictine humility when the building committee cochair confronted me, but I was not. I was merely humiliated by my duplicity. Grace led this lay leader to not lord it over me. By getting down on his hands and knees to help in the undoing of the carpenter's work—work that I had secretly and sneakily directed—he allowed me to be humbled without being humiliated.

Trust is our basic currency in the parish. It takes years to develop it, and in a few short moments it can be gone through disobedience. Our modeling of obedience to the Great Narrative of Redemption is the foundation of developing trust in the people we lead. They need to trust us. They might disagree with us from time to time—they may even be angered by a sermon we preach or position we take on an issue—but they will trust us if we model obedience, if we are in the regular practice of listening to God's word, to the Church's prayers, and to our neighbor's voices, who like us are attending themselves to discipleship in Christ.

I remember the event like it was yesterday, even though it is now nearly two decades ago. I am glad I remember it in the same way I do all the times I have been disobedient to my calling. Each is a reminder to me of what my disobedience can do when I am in a leadership position. When I fail to listen to what I know is true, when I do what I know is wrong, then I risk potential damage to the work of Christ.

My Obedience

When I became rector of a particularly large urban parish, I had little idea of what I was stepping into. I thought I did. I had been ordained long enough to know better, but I did not ask enough good questions in the search process. I had no idea of the pent-up anger in the parish, nor the voodoo economics that governed the parish budget. When I had been in place for a couple of months and started to pay attention, I realized that the budget was unsustainable; we did not have the pledges to support it and we were drawing down on both the parish reserves and the endowment fund to cover current expenses. The reserves were nearly gone and the endowment, which had once been well over a million dollars, was under $250,000 and going fast. I presented the vestry with my analysis. While I saw many of them nod their heads in agreement, others seemed tentative to make any changes to our expenses. It meant dismissing staff and cutting back on service ministries and other highly valued ministries. I agreed it was not going to be pleasant, but pointed out the current budget had been put together with wishful thinking and was not based on reality. I asked if we could really expect our budget deficit to go away with any significantly increased giving in the short term. A member of the finance committee piped up, "Well, usually somebody dies." I did not know what he meant, so he elaborated, "In past years, we've made up the deficit by the end of the year with bequests from parishioners who died that year."

I was speechless, at first. I then said I knew this would be a tough pill for all of us to swallow, but that we had to model good stewardship for the parish; if we expected people to give generously in the years to come, they had to trust us in how we managed the resources we had. Though not enthusiastically, they agreed to a new budget for the coming year that necessitated staff downsizing along with other cuts in our expenses.

I should have anticipated the reaction, but I did not. The staff who were let go each had a constituency in the parish that was vocal in their displeasure. Other parts of the budget—music, community service—also had to be cut back and each of those areas had people who were outraged. I tried to respond to each burst of anger with calm reality. We did not have the funds to support all those expenses. When we saw more generous giving in the parish, then we would be able to restore many of those ministries. The trouble was many people thought the parish had strong pledged giving. We did not. Our median pledge was about a thousand dollars a year in an extended neighborhood whose median income was nearly a hundred and fifty thousand dollars a year. Pointing that out only made people angrier and I became the focal point for much of that anger.

In the wisdom that comes from hindsight, I should have insisted the vestry share in being on the receiving end of the anger (obedience, after all, is not an individual *askesis*). But I wanted to be a noble martyr. That is what I thought being a good rector was all about. The first-year mutual ministry review turned into a referendum on me. It was not pretty. As each attack came, it hurt. I stayed connected to my spiritual director, colleague group, and bishop, seeking feedback from them and reassurance that I was leading on the right course. They all assured me that I just needed to stick with it and not run away. A little Benedictine Stability was in order, along with obedience.

As I listened to the words of scripture each day in the Office, I found myself drawn to the Psalms. Anyone who is experiencing martyrdom, or wants to be a martyr, finds them attractive. Many psalms depict one who is faithful to God while all those around are seeking their destruction. It was a trying time for me. If I had not been careful, I could have let myself engage in a bifurcated battle of Manichaean proportions where the forces of light (me) were fighting the forces of darkness (everyone who was attacking me). After all, I was right and those immature parishioners were just plain wrong.

My prayers would not let me go there, thank God. I decided to begin praying specifically for those who were angry at me—not for them to somehow realize they were wrong, but for them to know more fully the grace and mercy of God. My prayers, unfortunately, did not change their behavior, but something changed in me. I was able to take a less defensive stance around the parish's stewardship. I managed not to take the reactions so personally. To be honest, it is impossible not to take such reactions personally when you are under attack, but it gave me a stance and perspective where I could stand in a (relatively) nondefensive place. The daily prayer of the Church also helped shape me into one who would not get dragged into that bifurcated battle. I not only refused to get overly defensive, I also simply refused to return in kind what I was receiving. It took enormous discipline on my part because I so wanted to fight fire with fire. Oh, the things I said to myself about some of those people. My wife, Kelly, got an earful too. But grace prevailed. By my obedience to what I knew was right—the right stance to take in pursuing the right course—I was able to weather the storm.

Some of the more strident and angry people left. Others withdrew. In their place grew a stronger lay leadership who were committed to the conviction that responsible stewardship would lead in the long haul to greater generosity and stronger ministry. When I left that parish for another call, the endowment was nearly two million dollars, our ministry in the community had grown, a modest reserve fund had been restored, and the parish budget remained balanced. After the good-bye party for my family and me, one of the lay leaders came to me privately and said, "Thank you. Throughout all these difficult years I saw you take hit after hit after hit. I kept waiting for you to hit back and you never did. That made me see things about the church that gave me hope. If you could do that, then maybe I could do that too."

He will never know how much that meant to me. He gave me grace at that moment that put the past difficult struggle into greater perspective. It was worth going through all that. Obedience is its own reward.

The "Trivial Round" of Obedience

When I was first ordained, I thought obedience to the Great Narrative of Redemption would be only about grander, more spiritual things. I thought I would lead people in more obvious ways to deeper faithfulness and discipleship. But Keble's "trivial round," exemplified in the struggle over the parish budget, showed me that the more mundane things of parish life can have a profound effect on such faithfulness and discipleship. I also learned the truth of Jesus's words: "Whoever is faithful in a very little is faithful also in much; and whoever is dishonest in a very little is dishonest also in much" (Luke 16:10). And it is also true: we who are obedient in the mundane things of parish life will also be obedient when it comes to the big stuff. Likewise, if we cannot be obedient in the everyday leadership of the parish, then, when push comes to shove, we will not have the capacity to be obedient when the stakes are higher.

Obedience as Holy Listening

Parish life can be hectic at times. The urgent can mask the important. The problem in front of us at a certain moment can block the view of the larger vision to which God may well be calling. Obedience then serves us a great gift. It slows us down because it requires listening on so many levels: to scripture, to our prayers, and to the words of our neighbors in the church. We will often have to insist upon such obedience, because we serve a culturally infected Church, one that so often acts without listening to the many voices she needs to hear. Obedience insists that we first listen to God's voice in its different forms with one another, then humbly act, and then reflect critically on our actions. In our quick-fix-just-do-it-winning-is-everything culture, taking the needed time to be obedient is one of the greatest challenges of parish leadership. Yet, it is also one of the greatest gifts, if we accept it.

Our Context for Obedience

There has never been a time in the life of the church when obedience has not been a challenge for Christians. In our generation, however, we have learned more about why that may be true because we have learned more about the complexities of human behavior through scientific research. Recent studies acknowledge, for example, that people who are experts in a particular field tend to become rigid and unwilling to listen to alternative points of view related to their area of study.[5] This is even true, according to the research, for people who are not really experts at all, but were helped to feel they were experts by the study researchers. They, too, became more rigid in their thinking about their field of expertise and less likely to listen to points of view that differed from their own. The researchers referred to this as "belief perseverance," which is the tendency to stay with a certain belief even though the evidence suggests otherwise. It is also related to "confirmation bias," when one only interprets, favors, or recalls information that supports one's already held conviction. These insights frame just how hard it is to be obedient to the truth. Our own frames of reference are so distorted by a human tendency (see Francis Spuffurd's "human propensity to f**k things up," or HPTFTU[6]) that wants to avoid admitting we discerned wrongly or that limits what or who we listen to in order to discern wisely.

Admitting Our HPTFTU

I admit I suffer from this common human tendency. I engage regularly in HPTFTU. I would like to think, because I am so self-aware and tuned into the fact that I have unconscious bias and belief perseverance, that I would be above it all. Since I know what is happening inside of me and inside of other people, somehow none of this applies to me, which is what Stanley Hauerwas once called, "The Yale Way of Doing Things." He said when he was getting his PhD at Yale it was assumed that if you were in a group theological discussion and you could accurately describe everyone else's point of view, by default your point of view was the correct one.[7]

I like to think of myself as an expert on many things. Whether it is Anglican theology, baseball game management, the deficiencies of midcentury modern architecture, or the tragedy of Mark Richt's firing as the head football coach at the University of Georgia, I have an expert opinion. When I am honest with myself, however, I have to admit I am not an expert on any of those subjects. Still, part of me wants to believe I am. Our brains are wired for such a tendency. I have beliefs and views about each of the examples I listed. I have more learned beliefs in some over others, but truth demands my honesty. I am not an expert in any. For example, I have strong beliefs about the causes of the gun violence epidemic in our society. I cannot understand why we are doing nothing substantial to curb the wide availability of assault-style automatic weapons, which are clearly designed to kill lots of people quickly. It seems obvious to me what needs to be done: we need to get all these assault weapons out of the hands of all but the law enforcement community. Is it my belief perseverance that leads me to that conclusion? Do I have confirmation bias in that I am failing to seriously consider alternative points of view from my own when it comes to gun violence? I do not think so, but I cannot be sure. I try to listen to opposing views on this subject, but none of them makes any sense to me.

This is all part of our human sinfulness. We want to believe that our views and beliefs are superior, that our judgment is more insightful. I know my own tendency when other people challenge a belief I hold. Rather than consistently exercising Benedictine obedience and listening deeply to what they say, I sometimes ignore them as they speak, do not listen to a word they are saying, and begin rather to formulate a rebuttal to their position. Such spiritually immature behavior is the norm for all of us unless we discipline ourselves to respond differently. This is a lifetime task. I am still working on it.

The only medicine I know that can counteract this tendency is

God's grace. Resting in the grace of Jesus gives us the courage to discipline our immature reactivity. If we trust that God has reconciled the world through the Cross of Christ, then when our beliefs or views are challenged, we do not need to react to somehow prove our convictions are superior. We do not have to prove anything.

Jon Katz in his delightful book *Running to the Mountain*[8] tells of his own midlife crisis. He did not belong to any faith tradition (he was born Jewish), but he was experiencing a spiritual longing to discern a greater purpose to his life. He wanted to be obedient to that longing. He decided to buy a cabin on top of a remote mountain in upstate New York, live there, and listen to his life, or at least do his best to do so. He had to leave his (clearly quite supportive) wife, teenage daughter, and his home in suburban New Jersey. He ran to the mountain with his two Labrador Retrievers, Julius and Stanley, and the collected works of the monk Thomas Merton. The mountaintop experience turned out to be far more challenging than he had imagined. He dealt with a bitter, cold winter, battled a mice infestation in his cabin, and struggled with personal isolation. He also discovered a truth about his dogs. He had always thought that Stanley and Julius had been well trained. In suburbia they were models of obedience. He could take them walking off-leash on the hiking trails near his suburban home and they would always stay at his side. But on the mountain, he discovered they began to return to the wild. They would run after anything that held the promise of being food. He would call them and they would not come if they were on the scent of something to eat. This was a great shock to Katz. His dogs had become different animals once they were removed from the disciplined context of their lives.

Now, humans are not Labrador Retrievers. The Bible does call us sheep and we have enough in common with both Labs and sheep for this story to resonate with us. We know that when we stop listening to God in the scriptures, the prayers of the Church, and the voice of our neighbor, we stumble into disobedience and begin to lose touch with our baptismal identity and purpose in

Christ. We might not walk away. We might inch away. We might slide slowly away. We might even do all these things without even realizing they are happening. One day, hopefully, we will awaken and realize our disobedience.

There is a story told of two men walking down a crowded, noisy city street. In the midst of the noise of horns blaring, people screaming, and jackhammers chewing up pavement, one of the men stopped walking and said, "Did you hear a cricket chirping?"

The other man said, "What? Are you crazy? Who could hear a cricket in all this racket?"

Without saying a word, the first man took a quarter out of his pocket, threw it up in the air, and then stood back to see what happened. The quarter bounced on the sidewalk and then came to rest. Immediately, people stopped walking and looked for the coin. The first man smiled. "We hear what we want to hear."

We hear what we want to hear. That is our regular practice of disobedience. If we lose touch with the obedience to the God who called us by grace, we find ourselves listening to other voices that are all too ready to tell us what we want to hear, rather than what we need to hear. We who seek to lead congregations are as susceptible to disobedience as anyone else if we do not remind ourselves daily of the Promise of Obedience. The cacophony of voices that bombard us each day are not normally the voices of grace. They are voices of envy, shame, and pride, or they are the voices of over-functioning, workaholic self-justification. They are the voice of the Evil One. Without the discipline of obedience, we will listen to the often polluted sounds of the culture around us. It is easy to get distracted away from God's love and grace as we try to lead faithfully. When most of the voices we listen to are not the voice of grace, but that of the Evil One, we tend like everyone else to create God in our own image. If we are honest with ourselves, we all want a god who looks and acts like us. We want a god who shares our prejudices, proclivities, and politics. We want a god who agrees with us so we can rest easy knowing we are okay, while those who do not agree with us or act like us are bound for eternal judgment.

One of my favorite *New Yorker* cartoons shows an Episcopal priest (presumably) at the breakfast table with his wife, saying, "Darling, last night I had the most wonderful dream. I dreamt that God agreed with me on everything." I am sure God finds that more than a little bit amusing.

Reclaiming Obedience

The most powerful prophylactics against disobedience is an open, listening soul and people around us who love us enough to tell the truth about us as they see it. We must have the discipline to ask for feedback from such loving friends and colleagues. In a larger sense, we must always ask, "What does the Great Narrative of Redemption have to do with this decision? What does the weight of the scriptures have to say about a particular course of action? What would obedience to that Great Narrative look like in this case?" As our soul remains open and listening to God and to our neighbors, we must also listen to the prayers of the Church. What are those prayers saying about the present decision? What would those prayers look like if they were a part of this decision? As the Church has prayed these prayers for millennia, what shape do they have in what obedience would like in this case? Further, as we stand listening, what word is coming to us from our neighbors in the church? How is God present in the longings of their hearts right now? What has the community heard from God that would look and sound like obedience in the present moment?[9]

This is a way to reclaim the threefold process of Holy Obedience. Put simply, it is listening to God in the scriptures, in the prayers of the Church, and in the voices of those around us (and sometimes those who are not even fellow disciples).

NOTES

1. Quoted in the Rule of the Order of the Ascension, http://static1.1.sqspcdn.com/static/f/1124858/26280250/1433264322093/The+Rule+of+the+Order+of+the+Ascension+as+of+May+2015.pdf?token=2syc7l4RPN0W4ul47hBWovCaDZY%3D.
2. *The Rule of St. Benedict* (New York: Vintage Spiritual Classics, 1981), chapter 2.
3. Ibid., chapter 3.
4. Quoted in the Rule of the Order of the Ascension.
5. Shankar Vedantam, "Being Labeled an Expert May Contribute to Someone Being Closed-Minded," Hidden Brain: A Conversation about Life's Unseen Patterns, NPR, December 1, 2015, http://www.npr.org/2015/12/01/457974684/being-labeled-an-expert-may-contribute-to-someone-being-closed-minded.
6. Francis Spufford in his book *Unapologetic: Why, Despite Everything, Christianity Can Still Make Surprising Emotional Sense* (New York: HarperOne, 2012) creates this acronym for sin.
7. Dr. Hauerwas shared this brilliant insight into our humanity at a cocktail party he and I both attended.
8. Jon Katz, *Running to the Mountain: A Midlife Adventure* (New York: Broadway Books, 2000).
9. This is akin to applying the three-legged stole of Anglicanism: scripture, tradition, and reason. We listen to what God's word says to us in the Bible (scripture), we pray and then listen to the prayers of the Church that have always been prayed (tradition), and we listen to the voice of God in our neighbor, even when that voice may be contrary to our own, and then we work through that (reason).

5

THE PROMISE OF CONVERSION OF LIFE

> The new person is like a garment made to cover the individual believer. . . . It is impossible to become a new person as a solitary individual. The new person is not the individual believer after he has been justified and sanctified, but the Christian community, the Body of Christ, Christ himself.[1]
>
> —Dietrich Bonhoeffer

Our Context for Conversion of Life

I long to be that "new person" to which Bonhoeffer refers. I know his words are true. My conversion of life is inextricably connected to the conversion of the people in the parish and the larger Church around me. I neither exist in a vacuum nor can I be a "lone ranger" and remain above or beyond the life of the Church around me. The same is true of the larger culture in which we live. If we in the Church believe that we can somehow hermetically seal ourselves off from this larger culture, we are living a fantasy. While we are called to be in, but not of, the world (John 17:15–16), we have no choice. We might not belong to the world, as Jesus assures us, but it is the only one in which we may live. We are, therefore, steeped deeply in the culture and mores of this world.

As a man raised in the racism of my age, there is no greater challenge for conversion of life than seeking to overcome my own racism. My paternal grandfather was a member of the KKK. He regularly used the N-word (although, after getting a stern talking-to by my mother, he stopped using it in my presence). I am not alone, of course. Every white person in my generation was raised in a racist culture. It was unavoidable.

Researchers at Stanford University have exposed just how deeply embedded racial constructs are in our culture today. The study "Race and the Fragility of the Legal Distinction between Juveniles and Adults"[2] asked participants to read about a fourteen-year-old male with seventeen prior juvenile convictions who brutally raped an elderly woman. Half of the respondents were told the offender was black; the other half were told he was white. The man's race was the only difference between the two stories. Participants were then asked two questions dealing with sentencing and perception. The first question was, "To what extent do you support life sentences without the possibility of parole for juveniles when no one was killed?" The second question was, "How much do you believe that juveniles who commit crimes such as these should be considered less blameworthy than an adult who commits a similar crime?" The study found that participants who had in mind a black offender more strongly endorsed a policy of sentencing juveniles convicted of violent crimes to life in prison without parole compared to respondents who had a white offender in mind.

The result hardly should be surprising given the racial history of our culture. What surprised me was that the study accounted for racial bias and political ideology. Since the study controlled for those effects, it was clear that neither accounted for the results. One of the study's authors said, "The findings showed that people without racial animus or bias are affected by race as much as those with bias."[3] This indicates how deeply seeded racism is in our culture.

Before the 2012 presidential election, Arizona Secretary of State Ken Bennett told a radio interviewer that it was possible he would keep President Obama off that state's ballot unless he received proof the president was born in the United States. "I'm not a birther," he said at the time. "I believe that the president was born in Hawaii, or at least, I hope he was."[4]

Secretary Bennett was a respected elected official in his state. He was well educated, accomplished in his life, and, in his own words, he disavowed any racial bias or participation in wild conspiracy theories. And yet, he said he might possibly withhold President Obama's name from the presidential ballot in his state. Maybe the Stanford study could help explain how Secretary Bennett could possibly consider doing that. I must wonder if it would have been something the secretary would have even remotely considered if President Obama had been white.

St. Benedict reminds us in his Rule that we are called to a daily process of conversion of life. Such conversion, however, cannot truly happen unless we are willing to have the full light of truth shine on us and on the culture in which we live. We are affected by our culture in ways that are so deep and unconscious we often have trouble recognizing the truth when it comes to us. This means, rather than berating ourselves for our bias, racial and otherwise, we would do better to keep awake to the reality that our lives are shaped and influenced by a combination of genes, experiences, and the ways of thinking in the community and culture in which we were raised. We can never unring those bells.

My own racism is still a work in progress when it comes to conversion. As a product of my generation and place, I can no more be free of racism than I can be free of my own skin. I can only repent of those things and the experiences I have had as I come to see them anew in light of the Great Narrative of Redemption. My conversion and amendment of life comes through God's grace that calls me time and again, even daily, to the conversion of my life. To be a disciple of Jesus, to be one who has thrown my lot in with the Great Narrative of Redemption, is to be one who is committed to conversion of life, both mine and others. Our vows in baptism give us identity and purpose so that our lives, our relationships, the Church, indeed the very culture in which we live, may be converted—that the kingdoms of this world will one day become the kingdom of our God (Rev. 21). By practicing stability and obedience, we are confronted with the truth about ourselves as we seek faithfulness to the Lord. The struggle in the world and the struggle in our souls are really one and the same. In the work of conversion, we are blessed to discover that God's kingdom is as close to us as our arm's length (Mark 1:15).

The *Askesis* of Conversion of Life

Daily conversion of life, then, is the *askesis* of seeking God's presence in the new thing, the next person, or the circumstances of our life today. It is always there as a possibility in the next moment and experience. Our bodies change as we age, the Church becomes different, a beloved friend dies. In life, we face continuous change, whether we welcome it or not. If our conversion of life is to be part of that change, we must seek amendment of life,[5] which is predicated on our prayers for an openness to the work of the Holy Spirit in our lives. The scriptures refer to this as an openness to joy. In that joy we are "straining forward to what lies ahead" (Phil. 3:13). We live joyfully, trusting that God is in the next moment. There are ways for all of us to take and maintain a stance of openness to the grace of God breaking into our lives. Grace converts us. We cannot make it happen, but we can work to place ourselves in position to receive it.

Openness to Conversion of Life: Living in the Present

One of the most profound books I have ever read is *I'll Quit Tomorrow: A Practical Guide to Alcoholism Treatment* by Vernon E. Johnson.[6] As the title suggests, alcoholics can delude themselves into thinking that they can just put off quitting drinking until the next day. We all live in that delusional place to some extent. I will exercise more starting tomorrow. I will eat better tomorrow (but I will eat this dessert now). I will get more sleep. I will be more loving to my spouse. Whatever it is, we speak of our conversion in the future, which absolves us from facing today.

We face the same thing in our parish leadership. We find ourselves dreaming about how we will do things differently in the future, or how we will be a better leader when we are called to a better parish. I know we have all had those fantasies. My ministry is always better when I conceive of it in the future at a different parish with different parishioners. There it will be wonderful. I will have the resources I need to lead the people to great things. In that future, my parishioners will be so compliant with my vision that they will flock through the doors just to hear me speak. Such fantasizing is normal. It may even be a healthy counter to a rough patch we are going through. When I was in such a tough place in my parish ministry, I received a call out of the blue from a local nonprofit ecumenical ministry. The caller said the board of directors had given him the task of finding their next executive director. He had done his homework and talked to many people. He was convinced I was the right person to present to the board. And, by the way, the salary was double what I was making in the parish. I declined further discernment with them, but it was restorative for me to hear that at least one person thought I had some gifts when it seemed to me, at the time, that no one in the parish thought so.

No conversion of life happens in the future. It happens as we give ourselves daily to the demands and possibilities we find. It is now and here, in the people, things, and circumstances of our lives, that we might be open to conversion, which means striving to make the Great Narrative of Redemption incarnate in the here and now, not in some large, grand way, but in the *askesis* of each day. Conversion comes daily, as we open ourselves up to the thrust of grace in the chance meeting at a coffee shop, what that dying parishioner says to us as we pray with her, or in the laugh we share with the parish secretary over the dumb thing we just did. It is in these little things, if we are open, where we experience conversion of life.

Openness to Conversion of Life: Living with Our Own Death before Us

Archbishop Desmond Tutu once said, "If I stand out in a crowd, it is only because I am standing on the shoulders of others."[7] If anyone could claim attention for himself after what he had experienced and how he had led his people, then it would be Archbishop Tutu. But he knows himself only too well. He also knows that he picked up the mantle of freedom and justice from those who had gone before him and he was merely carrying it for his time. Others would follow. The same is true of Mrs. Fannie Lou Hamer, the great leader for justice and voting rights in Mississippi in the 1960s, who said, "When I die, I will be five feet, six inches closer to the Kingdom of God." (Mrs. Hamer was five feet, six inches tall, and she planned on falling forward and not backward when she died.)

Both Archbishop Tutu and Ms. Hamer humbly recognized how dependent they were on others, both those who came before them and those who came after them in the struggle for freedom and justice. They had their roles to play and they did not shrink back from their parts, but they were humble enough to see that their parts in the drama were only temporary—that, as Dr. King said, "The arc of the moral universe is long, but it bends toward justice,"[8] and they were merely the current workers seeking to bend that arc just a little bit more while they were on this earth.

It is good for us to experience a similar perspective and humility. I try to remind myself at least weekly that I am the tenth Bishop of Georgia. There was a ninth and there will be an eleventh. I am the steward of this holy office for the time being. Bishops come and bishops go. Such perspective brings with it humility. Some part of God's kingdom will come a little bit closer because of my ministry as bishop. Some part will stay distant. I will occasionally succeed in being the bishop God has called me to be and I will also, at times, fail miserably to live into that calling. It does no good to be fixated on what my legacy might be. If there is a story of my life, or of anyone's life who trusts the Great Narrative of Redemption, it is but a footnote in that one great and true story.

The amazing Broadway musical *Hamilton* is the story of the life of one of America's founding fathers, Alexander Hamilton. The musical ends with a mournful, chilling song that asks this question, "Who tells your story?"[9] We do not always get the opportunity to tell our own stories and what we tell will only be partial, for the impact of our lives must await someone else's judgment.

St. Benedict wrote in his Rule, "Keep your own death before your eyes each day."[10] He had no unhealthy fascination with death. For him, it was all about humility and learning to depend radically on God's grace and only on God's grace. This practice of keeping our deaths before us is liberating. It frees us from being held captive by the future, which we cannot control. It opens us up to the possibility of the present, whatever it is, that we may experience the work of God's grace in the present tense.

We should look to the future. We should help our people plan, strategize, and shape a parish life that conforms to the Great Narrative of Redemption, but in our own personal work we should be content with the day that God has given us. In doing so, we will help our people be content as well. When contentment comes and anxieties take a back stage, there is room for God's grace to convert us daily.

Openness to Conversion of Life: Living with Spiritual Maturity

When people ask me to pray for them, I want to readily agree. I keep their names in my briefcase and when I say the Daily Office I take them out and say each name, asking for God's mercy upon them. I will pray for people when they ask, but I also tell them I cannot pray *for* them. They must say their own prayers. I cannot say their prayers for them. If I do that, I infantilize my parishioners, stunting their own spiritual growth.

Years ago, I heard the confession of a graduate student who was working on his PhD in religion at the local university. I try not to have expectations of people before I hear their confession in the Rite of Reconciliation. I do try to help them prepare for the rite, so they understand the nature of the sacrament and what they might expect, but I try not to have expectations for the actual time of confession. As this young man in his mid- to late twenties went into the specifics of the sins for which he desired absolution, I found myself thinking, "How old is this guy? He sounds like he is twelve years old. By the time you reach his age, your sins ought to be a lot more significant to confess than what I am hearing." I certainly had more interesting sins by that age. I heard the rest of his confession, pronounced absolution over him, and we embraced. As we were walking out of the chapel, I asked, "I'm just wondering. Before today, when was your last confession?" He replied: "Oh, it was a while ago. It was right before I was confirmed by the bishop at age twelve, I believe."

Bingo. In the dozen or so years since his last confession, he had not done much work on his life. The last time he had reflected on his sins and confessed them he was twelve. I wondered then if his academic pursuit of a doctorate in religion was his way of doing that work. I later spoke to him about it. I was heartened by the fact he received my feedback openly, and we worked together on a beginning Rule of Life for him so he could begin to take greater responsibility for his spiritual life and not cede it entirely to the liturgy of the Church.

Opening ourselves to conversion of life means committing ourselves to seeking maturity in our faith. Those who are ordained to lead God's people are expected to be of mature faith. We have done the work. This is particularly true for clergy. We have gone to seminary and been evaluated by the faculty there. We have been reviewed by the bishop, the Commission on Ministry, and the Standing Committee. We have checked all the boxes by undergoing physical examinations, psychological examinations, and years of spiritual direction. Yet, I often encounter fellow clergy who have not experienced much spiritual maturation after all that work. My hunch is we have not taken the task seriously enough. Like the religion graduate student whose confession I heard, we often assume we are spiritually mature because we have endured all the prescribed work. Not necessarily so. In psychotherapy, a person only gets the benefits from it based on the level of their ownership and engagement in the work. Spiritual maturity requires us to take similar responsibility for our own spiritual growth and our development into spiritually mature people. Woody Allen famously said, "Eighty percent of life is just showing up."[11] We must show up when it comes to our own work of spiritual maturity.

Becoming spiritually mature does not equal arriving at sanctification. That is a gift from God that we cannot manufacture ourselves. Rather, it means owning our own stuff, saying our own prayers, confessing our own sin, making amends to other people when we have hurt them, telling ourselves the truth about ourselves before we tell other people. Being a child of God does not mean we behave or think of ourselves in childish ways. A radical dependence on God's grace frees us from a fear that prevents us from asking ourselves the hard questions and then demands that we not run away from the truth of the answers. God can handle the truth about us (the Cross and Resurrection confirm that), so we are liberated to pursue it ourselves.

The role model for us in this work of spiritual maturity is Augustine of Hippo, who in his *Confessions* lays bare his soul and is unafraid to ask the spiritually difficult questions his life presents. One story he tells is about a time when, as a teenager, he and some friends scaled the wall of a neighbor's pear orchard. While there, they picked a pear tree clean of its fruit. Augustine says his group did this "not to eat the fruit ourselves, but simply to destroy it." Why did he and his friends engage in such pointless destruction? Were there double dares declared? For Augustine, the answer for why he did such a thing was clear: his inherent human sinfulness. He was willing to do the hard work of spiritual introspection, to ask the hard questions of himself.[12]

A few years ago, Brian Williams, then the NBC Evening News anchor, was pilloried in the media for telling lies about his record as a television journalist in Iraq during the war and in New Orleans after Hurricane Katrina. He apparently embellished his record, citing deprivations and dangers that were simply false. We never learned how he felt about these embellishments. His response to being exposed never was quite confessional. He never said why he felt he needed to misrepresent his résumé. Why would someone who had achieved all he had feel a need to lie about his record? My hunch is there was something inside telling him that what he had achieved was not good enough, that embellishing his résumé made him more honored and revered, that the lies he told would assure that people would see him as a person of depth and gravitas. Williams is more like us than we may care to admit. His actions show an insecurity caused, no doubt, by a deep spiritual immaturity. He needed to falsely build himself up to feel important and valued by his peers. If that does not sound familiar, then participate in an average clergy gathering.

There you will hear all about the wonderful successes of those gathered. You will hear them try to build up their résumés in the eyes of their peers, all to appear more than they are. I know whereof I speak. I have been there and acted that way myself.

God's grace is more than sufficient for all of us. Opening ourselves to a conversion toward greater spiritual maturity means learning to rest in that grace. Spiritual maturity comes as we jettison the need to be seen by others as spiritual or leadership giants. When we accept God's acceptance of ourselves, which is grace, we can then take responsibility for ourselves as we are and not as we want others to believe. This is the beginning of spiritual maturity. When we practice it in the *askesis* of our leadership, it frees up the whole parish to be truthful people.

Openness to Conversion of Life: Living with Emotional Maturity

Being open to conversion in our emotional life means accepting responsibility for ourselves so that we might love others rather than blame them for whatever dissatisfaction we have with our own lives. Such blaming is the root cause of so much sadness and destruction in human relationships, especially in the church. We, as clergy, get blamed when there are not more people in the pews or when parish life is in some way mismanaged. We blame the laity for not being willing to try anything different to get the parish unstuck from its present course, or for not supporting us enough in the impossible vocation we have. Blame goes all around and it feeds on itself. It becomes akin to a circular firing squad.

Seeking conversion of life to greater emotional maturity means we will have egos strong and secure enough that we do not need to blame others—whether it be the laity, the bishop, or the larger Church—to absolve ourselves. This level of maturity is called differentiation. It is the ability

- to not get hooked into the emotional state of others;
- to stand outside a relationship with some detachment that allows us to practice empathy, which engenders compassion; and
- to have a place to stand where there is a clear delineation of personas.

Differentiation allows us to be individuals while also acknowledging the reality that we are relational creatures like everyone else. If we err by being too individualistic, we deny the reality of our position of leadership in the human relationships within the parish. We discount the depth of our own sin. Our understanding of sin then becomes too weak (remember HPTFTU?). We scapegoat others by identifying another person as the sinner, the one responsible for the problems of the parish. Humans are multiply conjoined. We are never completely autonomous.

Likewise, if we err by losing our individual identity, we lose the capacity to take responsibility for our lives. This too can result in scapegoating. So, if we go to either extreme, we lose our capacity to function in an emotionally healthy way, both in our families and in the people we serve. When we are emotionally healthy, we live creatively in the tension between the extremes. We maintain our individuality while recognizing our inescapable role in shaping the human relationships within the parish.

We need to be aware of our own emotions and how we can be tossed to and fro by them in parish ministry. Our work to reach emotional maturity will open us to conversion of life. It will help us keep a perspective on ourselves that is truthful while also being forgiving. We will learn to have compassion for ourselves when we find our buttons pushed and are tempted to react immaturely. It will also allow us to have compassion for others who do the same. Emotional maturity helps us remain open to what God is doing in the present and what grace may be imparted.

Openness to Conversion of Life: Living a Real Life

> My life shall be a real life, being wholly full of Thee.
>
> —St. Augustine, *Confessions*

> [The world is] full of phonies.
>
> —Holden Caulfield in *The Catcher in the Rye*

Historically, in our culture, people have turned to Augustine to read about a life well examined and well lived. At some point, Holden Caulfield became a more popular source for such meaningful introspection and living. It is an irony of our time that Augustine is a real person and Holden Caulfield is a fictional creation of J. D. Salinger. But the irony is deeper than that. For many today, church leaders are the last people they will think of when they look for someone who is truthful, realistic, and hopeful. There are many reasons for this. Certainly, news stories of church leaders behaving badly have not helped people see in us signs of hope and the expectancy of grace. We can bemoan this loss, or we can get on with trying to live a real life. In our own lives, and in how we stand within the community, we can call ourselves and others to a real life, the kind Augustine wrote about. When people meet us for the first time, do they find someone who is expectant and hopeful, or do they see a person who stands in a caustic or cynical place? Do they get from us a sense that we expect grace to govern our life and future? In the language of the Bible: Do people see in us a glimpse of hope for the coming of God's Holy City? Do they get an inkling of what God has intended all along for God's creation? Do they experience grace emanating from us so that they might find themselves drawn into the very life of Jesus?

This is not a backdoor call for our perfection. If you have read this far, you know that is not where I am going. I am, however, suggesting that the attitude we have about life will naturally show itself in the people we are called to lead. If we are truly grounded in God's grace in Jesus, then we will exude such grace and expect that grace will prevail as the kingdoms of this world become the kingdom of our God. It matters not whether we are introvert or extrovert, or any of the various personality types described in categories created by inventories like the Myers-Briggs. It is not about the giftedness we have or do not have. It is not about us needing to have a certain personality type. It is about the hope that is in us and whether those we lead can see that hope in us.

Holden Caulfield was right—at least in his contention that the world is full of phonies. Well, maybe not full, but full enough that people today take a much more cynical stance in their lives. They are turned away by what they see as the phoniness and hypocrisy of the Church. And the Church bears her fair share for why people feel this way. Yet, people are still longing in their lives for truth, hope, and meaning. If we remain open in our own lives to the constant conversion that grace imparts, we will manifest that hopeful grace in our interaction with the people, things, and circumstances of our lives. Because of the grace God has imputed to us, we will be comfortable in our own skins. We will be really real with others because we have been really real with ourselves. We will have hope that God will use us as we are, with the gifts, skills, and shortcomings we have. Because of that hope, we will be able to invite others to the same *really real* life, one that fully expects God, in the words of Dame Julian of Norwich, to "make all things well."[13]

Openness to Conversion of Life: Living with Our Own Anxiety

Anxiety is a powerful driver of human behavior. Just google "anxiety disorders" and see how many hits there are. Anxiety, and the fear it produces, can lead us into all manner of behaviors, most of which, upon reflection and self-examination, do not draw from us a strong testimony to God's grace and providence in our lives.

We live in a time when political and business leaders use our anxieties as weapons in their arsenal. They know we are anxious about terrorism, economic security, and health care, so they play on those anxieties, reassuring us that if we elect them, or invest in them, that all our anxieties will dissipate. Some religious leaders do much the same thing, but the anxieties they play on are a bit different, though not unrelated. If we are anxious about our soul's eternal destination, then they have a prescription for us. All we must do is believe as they believe. If we have anxiety about our relationships, then they tell us how to end those anxieties by following biblical principles. If we are anxious about whether God loves us and wants us to prosper, then they have a prosperity gospel to sell us. Those who manipulate our anxieties want us to believe that God will be outflanked by what is wrong with the world. That is such a weak god. It is the god of the functional atheist. It is not the God we meet in the Bible. The God and Father of our Lord Jesus Christ is not stumped by our sins or anything else, including our anxieties.

I am not saying there is anything wrong with having anxiety. It is a natural human experience. Our anxieties are not always illegitimate. They can be important canaries in the coal mine for us, letting us know that we are facing a real challenge and that we better prepare. It is how we handle our anxieties that matters. Do they cause reptilian reactions from our souls or do they encourage in us the higher soul-functions of hospitality, compassion, and generosity? Anxiety that goes unexamined and is not showered with God's grace can lead us to become de facto functional atheists. Functional atheism means we give assent to God's grace-filled providence with our lips, but we actually live our lives as if we were not part of a divinely coherent story that is moving the world toward God's plan of salvation. The gospel is clear about the world God created. John writes, "God did not send the Son into the world to condemn the world, but in order that the world might be saved through him" (John 3:17). When we open ourselves up to the thrust of God's grace in all things, our anxieties do not magically disappear, but they are placed in the context of God's providential grace for the world. We, who live our lives holding both our anxieties and our faith in the providence of God, will experience an effective antidote to functional atheism.

God is in the business of reconciling and restoring the world through the merits and mediation of Jesus Christ. The world is not a random, meaningless place. It is God's world full of love and meaning. That does not mean the world is perfect. We know better. It is full of sinners like you and me. It does mean there is a *telos* to the world rooted in and underwritten by God's providence. It should not surprise us, then, that the most recurring words of Jesus in the Gospels are, "Don't be afraid." For us to lead well and remain open to our continuous conversion to a life of grace, we must learn to relieve ourselves of the various anxious attempts we make to ensure our future. We must reach a place where we confess it is God's business to decide how long God will use us. That is not fatalism. It is reality, if we truly place ourselves in the hollow of God's hand.

Openness to Conversion of Life: Welcoming Vulnerability

The daily experience of conversion of life will always require us to have an openness and vulnerability to the other and to the new thing that God is doing in our lives.[14] In parish ministry, it takes discipline on our part to maintain such openness and vulnerability, which rarely comes easily or naturally. If we can maintain such discipline, however, we will discover that our leadership will become less about us and more about what God is up to in the world through our ministry.

Vulnerability is the last *askesis* I address in this chapter, and it may well be the most important. Brené Brown has written provocatively on the "power of vulnerability."[15] It can have the exact opposite effect that we might think, based on the cultural constructs we have inherited. Our culture would have us believe if we show vulnerability, people will exploit us and run over us. My own experience tells me that is not true. When I have allowed myself to be vulnerable to others I have sought to lead in the parish, it has created an opposite effect. It has invited them to be vulnerable with me and with one another. When I have shared experiences of my own failure, it has unleashed in others a willingness to share their own failures. Such sharing creates space for a deeper bond of friendship and trust to grow.

I am not referring here to emotionally dumping all our experiences of sin on others in the church. That would be immature and potentially manipulative. What I am referring to is an openness to our own life experiences and willingness to share them appropriately. When I have done so, it has helped me become a more credible leader and more trusted by others. It is risky, because when we are vulnerable, some may choose to exploit our failings. I recall a sermon I preached when I used a vivid example of how I had once behaved as a Pharisee of the worst kind with a stranger who approached me for help. The story did not show me in a good light, let's just say. Most people were invited through that story to reflect on their own pharisaical behavior, but one parishioner used it for years afterward as proof I was not a worthy parish priest for the congregation. ("After all, he admitted he was a Pharisee.") Yet, I do not regret that or other times when I have been willing to be vulnerable to the people I led in the church. It, however, must be authentic to who we are and to our own experience, otherwise it will come across as spiritually immature. Nothing I have experienced as an ordained leader in the Church has been more edifying for my leadership.

NOTES

1. Quoted in the Rule of the Order of the Ascension, http://static1.1.sqspcdn.com/static/f/1124858/26280250/1433264322093/The+Rule+of+the+Order+of+the+Ascension+as+of+May+2015.pdf?token=2syc7l4RPN0W4ul47hBWovCaDZY%3D.
2. Aneeta Rattan, Cynthia S. Levine, Carol S. Dweck, and Jennifer L. Eberhardt, "Race and the Fragility of the Legal Distinction between Juveniles and Adults," PLoS ONE 7. no. 5 (May 2012): doi:10.1371/journal.pone.0036680, http://web.stanford.edu/~eberhard/downloads/20120523-RaceAndTheFragility.pdf.
3. Ibid.
4. Keith Koffler, "Arizona Secretary of State Threatens to Remove Obama from the Ballot," White House Dossier, May 18, 2012, http://www.whitehousedossier.com/2012/05/18/ariz-secretary-state-threatens-remove-obama-ballot/.
5. "Conversion of life" is the inner working on our will through our experience of grace. "Amendment of life" is the specific amends we make from the grace-fueled experience of conversion. Together they form the *askesis*.
6. Vernon E. Johnson, *I'll Quit Tomorrow: A Practical Guide to Alcoholism Treatment* (New York: HarperCollins, 1990).
7. Quoted in the Rule of the Order of the Ascension.
8. "Theodore Parker and the 'Moral Universe,'" All Things Considered, NPR, September 2, 2010, http://www.npr.org/templates/story/story.php?storyId=129609461.
9. "Who Lives, Who Dies, Who Tells Your Story," from the musical *Hamilton*, music, lyrics, and book by Lin-Manuel Miranda, 2015.
10. *The Rule of St. Benedict*, chapter 4.47.
11. Susan Braudy, "He's Woody Allen's Not-So-Silent Partner," New York Times, August 21, 1977, Section 2: Arts and Leisure, 11.
12. *The Confessions of St. Augustine*, trans. John K. Ryan (New York: Doubleday, 1960), book 2, chapter 6, page 72.
13. The Rt. Revd. Graham James, Bishop of Norwich, "All Shall Be Well," 2012 Julian Festival Address, The Order of Julian of Norwich, accessed September 18, 2017, https://www.orderofjulian.org/Article_-_All_Shall_Be_Well.
14. I am indebted to the Rule of the Order of the Ascension, which inspired much of this chapter's broad outlines.
15. Brené Brown, *The Power of Vulnerability: Teachings on Authenticity, Connection and Courage*, 1st ed. (Louisville, CO: Sounds True, 2012), audio CD.

6

ASCETICAL LEADERSHIP

Justin Lewis-Anthony's book, *You Are the Messiah and I Should Know: Why Leadership Is a Myth (And Probably a Heresy)*,[1] wins my award for the longest book title. His previous book was titled *If You Meet George Herbert on the Road, Kill Him*.[2] He has the provocative title thing down cold. In that previous book, he challenged readers to redefine how clergy should lead their congregations (the title gave away his basic thesis: clergy should not pastor a parish as George Herbert did). I thought it was a marvelous reflection on the leadership stance and approach clergy should avoid. In his second book, however, he creates a leadership straw man as defined in Western culture (a whole chapter on John Wayne alone, oh my!), and then he proceeds to tear down that straw man. Okay, I get it.

Lewis-Anthony reflects an understanding of leadership similar to that of the Occupy Wall Street movement: to wit, leadership is, by definition, a bad thing (or in Lewis-Anthony's case, a heresy). I am the first one to agree that many leadership practices, past and present in the Church, are wrong-headed and do not reflect the virtues of God's kingdom as declared in the Great Narrative of Redemption, but the reason the Occupy Wall Street movement fizzled and the reason many of our congregations are not thriving is not because leadership is a heresy. Rather, it is because our leaders are not equipped with the requisite skills to lead effectively in a post-Christian context, a context that requires them to jettison their role as a chaplain to a declining Church. Though Lewis-Anthony is on the right track and is a marvelous writer, leadership is not a heresy. It is just often misguided and misdirected in congregations.

Part of the problem with clergy leadership is how clergy are formed. Seminaries are still training clergy to serve congregations that rarely exist anymore (in the dictionary, see Episcopal Parish, Lake Wobegon). New clergy are not sufficiently prepared to serve most of our congregations in the twenty-first century. Most seminary professors have little personal experience in effectively leading congregations, so they serve up mainly an academic/theory approach rather than one that is balanced by experience, reflection, and action. Those who are in training (*askesis*) for clergy leadership should have the experience and capability to do what they are primarily called to do.

Seminaries also have little accountability in the Church-wide system for the clergy they produce. Until there is major accountability (and a Church–seminary agreement on outcomes), there will be no change. We simply cannot afford to have another generation of clergy who are trained to be congregational chaplains and grief managers for further decline. Yet, to send new clergy into parishes armed with post-Christendom theories alone will not suffice either. Those leading congregations need to have the spiritual depth and practical training to resist the chaplaincy role thrust upon them by congregations who just want their priest to take care of them. They also must have the emotional and spiritual maturity to know what they will face in terms of their parishioners' fear and grief around the cultural changes we are all experiencing.

While many laity do not believe they have changed their expectations of their church experience, they have. It has become more commodified. It has become a way for some people to create lives where their contentment and happiness are of prime importance. The demand for chaplaincy will only increase. We need parish clergy who will not get sucked into that role even as they understand the human dynamic involved.

In the Gospels, Jesus seems quite unconcerned with his disciples' contentment and happiness, or even if they have the correct doctrinal position. Rather, he is most concerned that they inculcate in themselves God's one-way love,[3] which we call grace, and then live sharing that one-way love in their lives. To make this crystal clear, Jesus incarnated God's one-way love on the Cross. We need clergy who will offer one-way love leadership.

The Primary Role of Parish Leaders

As I wrote in the introduction:

> Church leaders are those who stand with the people of God bearing the Great Narrative of Redemption in Jesus Christ. As stewards of this Great Narrative, all that they say and do should proceed from the Divine Truth that in the Cross of Jesus, God has redeemed and reconciled humanity.

This is the primary role of leaders in the Church. Everything else must be subordinate to the bearing and stewarding of that Great Narrative. When we confuse our role in favor of becoming CEOs, community organizers, therapists, political activists, or social activity directors, we lose our prime identity and purpose. To be sure, leading by good administration, community engagement, open-hearted listening, and community building are vital additions to this primary role, but they should never supersede the role of bearing and stewarding the Great Narrative. How do we begin to do that? Read on.

Congruence with the Personal and the Public

A well-known comedian performs a hilarious bit about flying first class now that he has become a successful entertainer and television star. He says when he is sitting in first class and sees a member of the military walking past him to economy class, he considers getting up from his seat and saying to them, "Look, you have been willing to serve and maybe die in your service on my behalf. Since you have offered such sacrificial service, the least I could do right now is trade seats with you so you can fly first class. Please, take my seat."

Of course, he never actually does this and probably never will, but he nevertheless jokingly contends that he is a better person, maybe even better than most people, for simply contemplating doing such a good deed. Most people, he asserts, would not even consider doing it. The well-known comedian is funny because his comedy captures the spirit of our contemporary culture, sometimes devastatingly so. In our culture, you do not have to act on your beliefs or convictions. To have a good life, it is sufficient just to have the right beliefs.

A few years ago, I asked an adult Sunday school class, "What are the expectations of a faithful Muslim?"

A few people immediately responded, "Pray five times a day."

Another quickly added, "Fast during the daylight hours of Ramadan."

Still another said, "If possible, make a pilgrimage to Mecca in your lifetime."

I then asked, "What are the expectations of a faithful Christian in our Anglican tradition?"

There was some awkward silence before one person offered, "Go to church on Sunday and try to live a good life." I saw a lot of nodding heads. Everyone seemed satisfied with that answer, but I said that in our Anglican tradition there were more behavioral expectations than that. I then spoke about weekly participation in the Eucharist, daily prayer using some form of the Daily Office, and the regular practices of service "to the least of these" and seeking justice in the world. And that was just for starters. I asked them to review the Baptismal Covenant in the Prayer Book. I said our Anglican Tradition had a Benedictine quality to its spiritual practice where we seek a balance of work, rest, and play; that we are strongly incarnational in living our faith, finding God particularly in the people, things, and circumstances of our lives. The general response was that this was all well and good, but none of these should be considered requirements or even expectations. One man even said it would not be very hospitable to newcomers if we laid expectations on them. "It might turn them off. They wouldn't feel welcome. Besides, we are saved by faith, not works." Yes, that is true. But faith, at least as I have always understood it, is more than going to church weekly and trying to be a good person. Faith is the joining together of belief and action such that it changes and shapes the way we live in the world.

As with the comedian's comedy bit, it is not enough for us, especially those who lead parishes, just to think good thoughts about God, or to intend with all our hearts to do good in the world, or to have the correct doctrine on all things. It matters that we do these things rather than congratulate ourselves for merely desiring to do them. Ascetical leadership begins with bearing and stewarding the Great Narrative of Redemption and it is operationalized in leading people to connect the faith of the Church with their life in the world, to help them develop a congruence with what they believe and the patterns and habits that shape their lives each day. It is practicing the things in our leadership that we have come to know produce the fruit of what it means to be a faithful church.

Since the Greek word *askesis* (ἄσκησις) literally means to "practice in order to refine," what might be our *askeses* as parish leaders that would lead to a parish church bearing the fruit of faithfulness?

Askesis of Empathy during Times of Change

One of the most important *askeses* for parish leaders is the gift of empathy for others, particularly those whom we lead. It is important for us to be able to place ourselves in other people's shoes, so to speak, and to try to understand what they are experiencing from their perspective. But having the gift of empathy for others is not all that is needed to lead a parish to become collectively more spiritually vital and healthy. Such leadership requires both a good knowledge of how change happens as well as the gift of patient determination.

Most of us have a pretty good idea of what a healthy Christian community looks like and acts like, but many of us are reluctant to lead congregations to incarnate such communal practices and norms. Why is that? We are rightly concerned that we might run afoul of individuals or groups within the parish who have a stake in maintaining an unhealthy status quo. In other words, people do not want their turf messed with, even if what they are doing is failing or ineffective. As a result, unhealthy practices around ineffective children's Christian formation, or music in the liturgy, or a community ministry continue because attempts to change them are understood as attempts to take away the authority of the Sunday school teacher or the organist or the community ministry coordinator.

Some of our leadership reluctance comes from a natural desire to avoid conflict. Conflict can be hard and unpleasant. Another part of the reluctance to make changes that would bring greater spiritual health to a congregation is related to our misunderstanding about the nature of change. We often mistakenly think people do not like change. That is not true most of the time. People do not dislike change, per se, but they will probably dislike any change they do not understand or a change in which they had no input. Also, if they cannot see the blessing the change could produce, they are not likely to even consider embracing it. Here is where our work of empathy comes in. If we exercise genuine empathy for the people who are being asked to accept a change, then the change has a good chance of succeeding. If those people are treated as obstructionists, or saboteurs, or are seen as "standing in the way of the gospel," then they are likely to dig in their heels and become real obstructionists or saboteurs. During such times, we must consistently stay in the role as leader, not withdraw, listen to all the voices in the congregation, and retain empathy for the people who oppose or question the proposed change. And we must do all that while not allowing those people to take over the agenda or control the emotional climate. That is a lot for us to handle and it takes real skill and training to negotiate it all well.

The *Askesis* of Balancing Task and Relationship

People are complex, amazing, exasperating, and funny creatures. If you doubt that, look in the mirror. We are able in one moment to engage in remarkable acts of love and devotion and then, in the next moment, to act in petty, vindictive ways. All this complex and exasperating behavior shows itself in our social interaction. Our interaction with others can produce in us both joy and anxiety, and yet it is fundamental to who we are as God's creatures. We drive one another nuts at times, but our neighbor is blessedly necessary for us. In theological terms, we might say that God has hardwired us to be in communion with one another.

David Brooks, the author and columnist, tells in his book *The Social Animal*[4] of a psychological research experiment (although he can't find a source verifying that it was ever actually done). In the experiment, middle-aged men were hooked up to a brain-scanning device. They were shown a horror movie while the device recorded the reactions in their brains. Later, they were hooked up to the same device when their wives were present. They were then asked to share their feelings with their wives. The researchers then compared the first and second brain scans. They were the same: complete terror during both episodes. I share Brooks's tale partly because I think it is hilariously true, but also because it illustrates our complexity and differences. And those are not just in terms of gender. Personality research and insight, such as produced by the Myers-Briggs Personality Inventory, informs us about our complexity and differences in how we take in and relate to the world around us. Some of us are innately introverted, while others are given to extroversion. Some think first and then feel second, while others feel first and then engage their thoughts. All this causes great challenges for us as we try to navigate the complexities of our myriad relationships in the church.

Maybe the most challenging difference we experience in community is the one related to the tension between accomplishing tasks and attending to relationships. This tension is a core challenge for leaders in the church. Some folks are task-oriented. When they are faced with a job to do or a role to live out, they just want to get it done. Others, however, attend themselves more to relationships. Accomplishing tasks is less important to them. That does not mean task-oriented people do not care about relationships or that relationship-oriented folks do not care about tasks. It means that in every community there will be people who tend to be more of one than the other. The key skill here is to help people stay on task while also helping them attend to the relationships in the group. God's mission is not well served if a certain task is accomplished but in doing so people are at each other's throats. Likewise, we will never engage in mission if we ignore the real tasks required to do so. If we wish to be effective, then we must be mindful of this basic reality and attend to it in every part of parish life. Both kinds of people are a part of every group within the parish. That's why parish life is never boring.

The *Askesis* of Learning from Experience

The organizational theorist Edgar Schein has studied for decades how organizations function, particularly around their specific culture's capacity to adapt to new learning in a changing context. His work with the Harvard Business School on these issues has gained him lots of attention among chief executives. He argues that there is an a priori contradiction in organizations: anxiety hinders the ability to learn, but anxiety is necessary if any kind of learning is going to occur. Anxiety about the way things are motivates one to learn something new, but anxiety has a negative cognitive effect on our ability to learn. We do not learn well when we are anxious. Schein goes on to argue that there are two kinds of anxiety associated with something new: *learning anxiety* and *survival anxiety*.[5] *Learning anxiety* is associated with the fear that we will fail at the new thing we are trying to do, or that it will be beyond our abilities, or that we will appear foolish to others, or that we must jettison our old patterns that used to work for us. *Survival anxiety* is the fear that if we are going to make it, to literally survive the context we are in, then we are going to have to change behaviors. In his studies of how businesses operate, Schein contends that most of the time *learning anxiety* is more powerful than *survival anxiety*. So, most people will opt to *not* learn new ways of business even though they know their professional survival depends upon it.

Schein's insights also apply to leadership of congregations. In a post-Christian context, we need to learn new ways of engaging God's mission to bring others to Christ and to serve people in our communities. We know we must do this, but we experience the learning anxieties that come from fearing that we might fail, or that we might not be gifted enough to do it, or that we might appear foolish to others, or that we might have to give up some of our old ways of doing things. So, what happens? Many congregations choose to die rather than to learn new missionary skills. Parish leaders face huge challenges here. Using Schein's constructs, how do we help people lower their *learning anxiety* so it is less determinative than their *survival anxiety*? One could argue that we could work from the other end by trying to increase survival anxiety, but that would be through the *via negativa*—increasing their fear that if they do not learn new ways of mission, then the congregation would die. I find that approach repugnant because it is based on threats and fear.

We need to create supportive opportunities for people to learn new missionary skills working with those in the congregation who have shown some motivation to learn. I think it is a mistake for us to expect everyone to overcome their *learning anxiety*, but we can work to develop a critical mass of willing learners—people who are ready, even if tentatively, to learn new ways of reaching out in mission. That seems to me to be a primary formational task for leaders in the church: identifying those disciples who are capable of learning new skills and then focusing our energy on working with them. Often, too much of our time and energy is spent on trying to get unwilling learners to learn. We may try to charm, cajole, or shame people into a learning mode. My experience tells me it is a profound waste of time. I am not saying these people should be ignored, but I am saying an inordinate amount of time spent trying to convince them to have a new learning stance is probably not effective.

There is a funny story told of a grandmother who took her grandson to the beach on a beautiful summer day. She brought everything they needed: blanket, umbrella, sand toys, and a good book for her to read. She laid out the blanket, put up the umbrella, and instructed her grandson to go play at the water's edge, but not to go in the water. With that, she began reading her book. Just a few minutes later, she looked up only to discover that her grandson was nowhere to be seen. She looked everywhere. Then, off in the distance, way out in the ocean, she saw him screaming and waving his arms. Her heart sank. She screamed, got up, and ran toward the lifeguard tower, yelling and pointing out to where her grandson was quickly beginning to go under the water and drown.

The lifeguard sprang into action. He grabbed his rescue sled, sprinted into the water, and swam out to the boy. The current was unusually rough and it seemed like hours before he reached him. Once he did, he placed the boy on the rescue sled and began the long, arduous return to the shore. When he arrived on the shore, a huge crowd had gathered to witness the dramatic rescue. The boy had been underwater for some time and was not breathing, so the lifeguard commenced with mouth-to-mouth resuscitation. Minutes passed, but the lifeguard kept at it. Finally, the boy coughed up the ocean water and began to breathe again. The crowd cheered. As the boy sat up, the lifeguard rolled to his side, exhausted. Every muscle in his body ached. He could not sit up, but he managed to prop himself up on his elbow and look up at the grandmother. She looked down at him and said, "He had a hat."

This story resonates with parish leaders. No matter what we do, or how hard we work, or how gospel-focused we are, someone is bound to say the equivalent of "he had a hat." In my experience, it is no good to reply, "Are you kidding me? Do you not know how hard I have worked and the sacrifices I have made in leading this church?" Some people will always choose to see our shortcomings rather than the work we have done for God's mission, especially if they are anxious.

To be sure, we should pay attention to our shortcomings. We should not dismiss criticism, especially when it is offered in a helpful way. We can, however, become too focused on those who say, "He had a hat." We are like the rest of humanity. We want people to like us and approve of our efforts when we work hard. But many of us seem to want everyone, and I mean everyone, to universally conclude we are doing an excellent job of leadership. We can become obsessed with winning over the "he had a hat" crowd. It is a fool's errand that leads to exhaustion and then resentment. Our efforts should go in the opposite direction. While not ignoring the "he had a hat" crowd or those with constructive criticism, we should spend most of our energy working with those who are not looking to see a dark cloud in every silver lining and who are willing learners of the *askesis* of the Church.

My experience tells me that many people in the congregation desire to learn the *askesis* of the Church and want to do so in partnership with their leaders. The "he had a hat" crowd, like the poor, will always be with us. Love them, care for them, but do not find leadership identity and purpose in them. They should not dominate our time and attention. In what may seem to some as counterintuitive, we ought to spend more time with those who show some openness to learn and grow and less time with the "he had a hat" crowd. If we have a high need to be loved and appreciated, then we will find this hard to do. We will want to try to win these people over, which is not likely to happen. What is most likely to happen is we will exhaust ourselves in the futile attempt to convince such people that we are worthy of their admiration and support. The only change likely to occur is exhaustion.

The *Askesis* of Trust Development

> If we . . . refuse to let the subject come into view, it may occasion suspicions, which, though not well founded, may tend to inflame or prejudice the public mind, against our decisions: they may think we are not sincere in our desire to incorporate such amendments in the constitution as will secure those rights, which they consider as not sufficiently guarded.[6]
>
> —James Madison to the House of Representatives, June 8, 1789

As this quote from Mr. Madison indicates, trust has always been an issue between people and the leaders of institutions. Today, such suspicions seem to be on steroids, and not without justification. The government spying on its own citizenry, financial institutions reaping questionable profits on shadowy deals with other people's money, worker productivity up by 90 percent in the last forty years but the percentage increase in their income during that same time only up in the single digits—all of this leads people to lose trust in public and private sector leadership and the institutions they lead.

Two recent books have proven this trend of trust erosion. The first is *New York Times* reporter Diana Henriques's book *The Wizard of Lies: Bernie Madoff and the Death of Trust*.[7] It describes how Madoff created the biggest Ponzi scheme in history. In a recent interview, Henriques said, "I think we're fooling ourselves if we think he's somehow unique or rare in our market environment. That's why I warn against seeing him as some sort of monster, some inhuman psychopath who arises and can't be stopped. He is not inhumanly monstrous; he is monstrously human."[8] The subtitle of Henriques's book is not hyperbole. People have lost trust in those who lead our institutions.

The second is James Stewart's book *Tangled Webs: How False Statements Are Undermining America*.[9] He claims we are becoming a society where perjury is the norm. He explores why people lie under oath and, consequently, how lives are ruined in the process. Lying, of course, is as old as the Garden of Eden (What tree? What fruit?), but today, people are lying at the highest levels of business, politics, and media. He examines the trials of Martha Stewart, Scooter Libby, Barry Bonds, and Bernie Madoff. He asks, Why do people with so much to lose by lying do so anyway? Why would Martha Stewart lie about receiving insider stock information? It was only $40,000 and she was a millionaire. His answer: like others, she had gotten away with things like this before and the lying simply became reinforced behavior.

From the Bible, we recall how King David deceitfully had Uriah killed so he could have Bathsheba as his wife. Why would he do such a thing? The answer the Bible gives is simple: he was the king and as such assumed the morality that applied to others did not apply to him. He was king. He could get away with murder.

It was not until Nathan confronted him that he confessed his sin and asked God's forgiveness. One wonders if such a confession ever would have occurred without Nathan's actions.

We live in a time in our society when, if trust has not died, then it's on life support. We must try to lead well in this context. Will anyone trust what we say? Will our actions be under constant suspicion? Even though we live in this toxic social environment, God is giving us an opportunity. We must insist on truthfulness and moral transparency on all levels, not in a self-righteous way or a way that conveys we smugly believe we are morally superior to everyone else, but in a humble way that lets everyone know we are committed to being a truthful people in Jesus Christ. Like everywhere else, the church has had our share of behavioral, financial, and other issues that have eroded trust. It does not matter if personally we have been free of such things, or that our congregation has not had some of these issues. We are all tarred with the same brush. Once someone loses trust in leadership, my experience says there is a one to ten ratio going on. For every year of mistrust, it takes ten years or more of hard work to recover it, which is why developing trust is never fully accomplished. It is always a work in progress.

Most people in our congregations now bring with them this current cultural suspicion, if not distrust, of leaders and institutions. There is an insightful video on YouTube that asks: "What If Starbucks Marketed Like a Church? A Parable."[10] It's a devastating critique of a visitor's first experience of church. I cringed when I viewed it because it rang so true to my observation of how visitors experience church in so many places. It continues to amaze me that people will return for a second visit.

When people come to church I believe there are three core steps to earn their trust.[11] First, they must experience *safety and acceptance*, which is common to anyone as they take part in a group. People will not stay in a group if they do not feel both safe and accepted. If they have children, then that concern is heightened even more. A good question to ask is, What about our experience in the congregation where we serve needs to change to meet this basic emotional and spiritual need of people for safety and acceptance?

The second step is *inclusion*. People, particularly newer people who have never been to church before, need to experience a sense that they are part of the group. So, during worship, when do they stand, sit, or kneel? Some people are crossing themselves, should they do that? Are they welcome at the altar? Which book do they use and when? When they look around and everyone else seems to be negotiating worship with ease, then it is hard for them to experience inclusion, and consequently they feel incompetent. No one likes feeling that way. It is why I do not play golf. I am incompetent at it. If I could play it better, then I would enjoy it. Helping people achieve a basic competence in our worship helps them experience inclusion. What about our experience in the congregation where we serve needs to change to meet this basic emotional and spiritual need of people for inclusion? One basic answer is for us to teach people how to worship in our tradition. We should not assume people know how to do so. Once they experience some basic competence in how to worship, they will naturally experience inclusion.

Another part of inclusion must happen if people are going to remain and grow in their *askesis* of the Church. After they have crossed the hurdle of inclusion enough to envision themselves possibly being a part of a particular Christian community, they must be able to imagine themselves as being able to offer who they are and the gifts they have to the parish. Too often, with the best of intentions, we do not invite people to offer their giftedness to the parish. We think we should not pressure them, but this undermines the inclusion process. We should ask: What do you enjoy doing? What are your interests? Then we should find a way to invite them into the work of the parish that most closely coincides with their enjoyment and interest. It is natural to all people's experience to want to feel they are contributing and making a difference in a group. Good questions to ask are: How does your church include people in this way? Must new people wait a few years before being invited? If so, they might not still be there.

The last core step is *trust development*. Once someone experiences safety and acceptance, and then inclusion, they are beginning to develop trust in the community, but that is not guaranteed. We still must earn the basic trust of people and then both develop and maintain it. When we practice financial opaqueness, make decisions without input or feedback, or make changes that appear arbitrary, we will undermine people's trust, especially those people who are relatively new to the congregation. They do not have a long enough personal relationship with us to mitigate such mistrust.

Empathy and the Golden Rule are powerful tonics to cure us of the above self-destructive behavior. Ask: if I were new to the congregation, what might help me better understand how we are stewards of financial resources here? How would I like to be included when it comes time to make a decision? What processes could we put into place so people would not perceive a change as merely arbitrary?

Put simply, such trust development is about maintaining the free flow of truthful information and a feedback loop that listens to the concerns of the congregation. This does not mean that no decision can be made until everyone agrees, but it does mean that we honor and respect everyone enough to be transparent and truthful in how we lead. Trust is the primary currency of every leader.

The *Askesis* of Humility

In an April 8, 2010, commentary in the *New York Times*,[12] David Brooks offered a powerful reflection on humility in leadership. While not writing for the church, his advice is spot on for how to lead in our church today. Brooks noted that most leaders in our culture are admired for their self-confidence and ability to project certainty about the future. But these leaders, Brooks wrote, have a short shelf life. They tend to burn themselves and others out quickly. In contrast, Brooks quoted Jim Collins, author of *Good to Great* and *How the Mighty Fall*. Collins said excellent businesses become excellent because they celebrate a different sort of leader—one who combines "extreme personal humility with intense professional will."[13]

His insight translates to how we should lead in the church. We need to spend less time in the spotlight and more time praying and strategizing with other leaders on how we might be more faithful and effective in sharing the gospel in our communities. Rather than "the sage on the stage," we need to be "the guide on the side," if you will pardon the rhyme. Are we intensely focused on sharing the gospel and inviting others to do the same? At the same time, do we do so with a sense of humility where we recognize that we do not have all the answers about the next step the parish should take?

The cocksure leader, Brooks argued, gets things done and makes things happen, but such a leader is ultimately destructive to the health of the organization because eventually others are not drawn into and invested in the success of the organization. They do not share the same stake. They are just following the orders of the one who gets things done and makes things happen.

Brooks referred to Collins again when he talked about the seductions that mark failing organizations: "The belief that one magic move will change everything; the faith in perpetual restructuring; the tendency to replace questions with statements at meetings."[14] In contrast, if leaders can stay true to their calling and remain open to the future, then they can avoid the power of that seduction.

The humble, yet focused leader is whom Brooks called for. Brooks ended his commentary with this: "If this leadership style were more widely admired, the country could have spared itself a ton of grief."[15] That's true for the church as well. In the church, we put way too much emphasis on having the right, carefully crafted mission statement. We redo our committee structures, believing that will do the trick. If we just do one huge thing—our "magic move"—it will change our course in the most positive direction. That is arrogance on our part. We make the mission about us and about what we want for the church and not about God's mission and God's desire for us.

The *askesis* of humility is always a challenge, but not overpowering if we keep in mind our own sinfulness and capacity for self-deception, which is usually a part of each of our blind spots. If we come to believe that our way is the only right way, or that our position on this issue or that problem is the only possible correct one, then humility will be hard to practice. St. Benedict states in his Rule that "self-will"[16] is the opposite of humility. Self-will, or we might say being self-focused, can keep us from a healthy *askesis* of humility.

Recognizing what is going on inside of us when we insist on our own way will help us acknowledge our own blind spots. The economist Daniel Klein calls this "my side bias,"[17] which is the tendency to judge ideas or information based on how conveniently they conform to our settled view of the world. I suffer from "my side bias" and so do you. We all do. Pure objectivity is not possible for anyone. We all bring to every idea or piece of information a subjective interpretation based on how we have come to see and comprehend the world. When we deny this self-deception in ourselves, we are perpetuating our own self-focused view of the world.

A partner to self-deception is self-delusion. It also hinders our *askesis* of humility. I do believe I approach my life and my experiences with others with the best of intentions. At least most of the time, I think I do. I know I want to believe I do. St. Paul's lament puts it in a related, but slightly different way: "I do not understand my own actions. For I do not do what I want, but I do the very thing I hate" (Rom. 7:15).

We all long for others to truly understand us. We want others to recognize that even when we "do the very thing [we] hate," we were not intending to hurt them, or make them angry, or cause them problems—or at least we think we were not. We all suffer from misunderstood motives, hurt feelings, and eroded trust in relationships that come from just trying to be understood, and even trying to understand ourselves and our own confused actions at times. St. Paul's shockingly self-revealing statement about himself reveals the truth about ourselves as well.

For hundreds of years in Western culture, we have sought to understand human identity and why we do the things we do. Some of our acts are acts of great compassion and courage, while other acts reveal what the Ash Wednesday liturgy of the Book of Common Prayer refers to as simply the "pride, hypocrisy, and impatience of our lives."[18]

Jonathan Haidt[19] and other moral psychologists have helped us understand all this better, but at the end of the day we are left with much of our human identity as a mystery to ourselves (Why indeed did I do the very thing that I hate? Maybe my intentions were not so good after all?). Like Maren Morris sings in her song, "My Church," we have all fallen down a few too many times. Self-delusion leads us away from humility. Humility helps us to recognize that our intentions, even during those times when they are good, can be occasions for the sin of self-will.

When we confess our "my side bias" and our capacity for self-delusion, we are exercising the *askesis* of humility. We are compelled to acknowledge that we are finite, limited creatures who get things wrong, often frequently. It can also aid us in our empathy toward other equally finite and limited creatures—the ones the Bible calls our neighbors. Such humility will help us develop and maintain generous hearts and open minds as we lead in the Church. We will learn to judge less and love more.

The *Askesis* of Transformational Change

> Start by doing what's necessary; then do what's possible; and suddenly you are doing the impossible.
> —Francis of Assisi

Every year, thousands of churches across the world hold annual pet blessing liturgies on St. Francis Day. There are the usual dogs and cats, less common animals like guinea pigs and ferrets, and the occasional exotic snake or two. I was always careful to keep my distance when asperging such exotic animals. You just never know how holy water might be received in such circumstances. I think it wonderful that the church holds such liturgies. It is a celebration of the whole of God's creation, something our brother Francis daily encouraged. Yet focusing only on this part of Francis's witness does not do justice to his genius as a transformational leader of the Church. Francis came to adulthood in the early thirteenth century in Europe when the Church seemed everywhere and nowhere at the same time. As an institution, it controlled vast wealth, but as a movement following Jesus it had grown poor. It was more concerned with keeping people chained to rules than liberating them through the Good News of God's grace in Jesus. It was like a big, old leaky barge still afloat going down the river, but it needed transformation.

Enter Francis. Whether he deliberately set out to be a transformational leader is unclear from the historical record, but he followed closely what has come to be known among organizational theorists as Gleicher's Model for Change,[20] which holds that change happens when there is a dissatisfaction with the way things are, a vision for the way things might be, and then the first few concrete steps toward that vision for change. If all those steps are greater than the resistance one will encounter, then the change will occur. Gleicher's Model for Change is written like this: $C = D \times V \times F > R$.

Francis first tapped into his personal dissatisfaction with his own life. By acknowledging his own dissatisfaction, he invited others to do the same with their lives. They did not need to go along with the way things were. But dissatisfaction alone produces grumbling and complaining. It never brings transformational change. Francis also had a vision for how things might be. What if we followers of Jesus sowed love where there was hatred, hope where there was despair, or pardon where there was injury? That was the vision Francis put before himself and the first folks who gathered around him. They then took steps to incarnate such virtues in their life together. Soon, others shared this vision and the movement grew. The old, leaky barge of the Church never did accept Francis's vision. In fact, he faced powerful resistance from bishops and princes who were threatened by such a simple vision for living the gospel together. While Francis didn't change the whole Church, he transformed some of it. His witness continues today. His vision calls us in the Church to become instruments of God's peace in all parts of our lives.

Leading ascetical transformation inevitably leads to some level of conflict in the Church. It is unavoidable. As we see with Gleicher's Model for Change, there will always be some amount of resistance to any effort to transform a system. Jeffrey D. Jones in his book *Heart, Mind, and Strength: Theory and Practice for Congregational Leadership*[21] addresses this reality quite well. He describes the clergy role as "adaptive leadership in conflict." In Gleicher's Model, we recognize that dissatisfaction is a part of everyone's experience in a system. I have used that reality in transformational work. When I was a parish priest in a new congregation, people would inevitably approach me stating they were dissatisfied about some aspect of parish life. Rather than try to argue with them, tell them they were wrong, or say they had unrealistic expectations for what the parish could do, I would say, "Tell me more about that. What specifically are you dissatisfied with?" By tapping into areas of dissatisfaction, we can redirect what may appear to be negative feelings into positive change. Of course, if we do not act to redirect the energy toward a vision for what might be, then dissatisfaction will spread and become toxic. Tapping into areas of dissatisfaction is a good way to encourage healthy conflict, and Jones contends parish clergy and lay leaders need to enhance, not reduce, conflict. Few of us enjoy conflict, but it is often necessary for any transformational change to occur. Our role in this *askesis* is to remain humble. We cannot be certain what exactly needs to be done. Remember, we are to lead by bearing and stewarding the Great Narrative of Redemption, and when that is applied to transformational conflict, it means creating a vessel of trust (inclusion, acceptance, and the free flow of information) so that the whole people of God can engage safely. It means sharing the work of transformation with the people, while maintaining the vessel of trust, so that the answers that emerge can be owned by the people. We should not create the conflict. It is already there. If we see our role as instigators, encouragers, or enhancers of conflict, then we deserve to suffer the consequences. That is not the role described here. What we should insist upon is that it come to the surface—to name the dissatisfaction and begin to cast a new vision of what might be. We can do this best, as I wrote above, by asking questions about the longings in people's hearts for the future.

Still, often a different approach is needed because of the capacity we all have for avoiding any form of conflict. When that is the case, we need to deliberately raise what everyone else is avoiding. This is equivalent to what has been called "naming the elephant in the room" or "getting all the snakes on the table." People will fear that any discussion of what they have been avoiding will provoke conflict. That is why we must maintain the vessel of trust. Creating this vessel of trust enables the answers needed for positive change to emerge. Truth be told, even when these safe parameters are in place, we will often have much of the uneasiness, resentment, and anger created by the conflict directed at us. Often, these emotional responses will show themselves as personal attacks. We need to be mature enough to not respond in kind. We need to know that even if it seems personal, it is not. It is simply the more immature among the congregation dealing with their anxiety. Keeping this perspective is crucial. In the words of Michael Corleone in *The Godfather*: "It's not personal. It's strictly business."[22]

It is not easy to develop this ability to distinguish between what is about the leader who is leading transformation and what is about the role they play in the system. It is the persistent challenge of parish ministry: being both person and symbol all the time. When under attack, it is almost impossible not to feel it personally. Reacting to attacks as personal will only make our role harder because, when doing so, we are agreeing with the attacker: it is about us. It also redirects the focus away from the transformation desired.

The *askesis* of transformational change becomes possible as we help people embrace their baptismal identity and purpose: "respecting the dignity" of others, "striving for justice and peace," and "loving our neighbors as ourselves."[23]

NOTES

1. Justin Lewis-Anthony, *You Are the Messiah and I Should Know: Why Leadership Is a Myth (and Probably a Heresy)* (New York: Bloomsbury Academic, 2013).
2. Justin Lewis-Anthony, *If You Meet George Herbert on the Road, Kill Him: Radically Re-Thinking Priestly Ministry* (New York: Mowbray, 2009).
3. My thanks to my friend the Reverend Paul Zahl for coining this highly accurate and descriptive term: one-way love.
4. David Brooks, *The Social Animal: The Hidden Sources of Love, Character, and Achievement* (New York: Random House, 2012).
5. Diane Coutu, "The Anxiety of Learning," *Harvard Business Review*, March 2002, https://hbr.org/2002/03/the-anxiety-of-learning.
6. https://founders.archives.gov/documents/Madison/01-12-02-0126
7. Diana B. Henriques, *The Wizard of Lies: Bernie Madoff and the Death of Trust* (New York: St. Martins Griffin, 2012).
8. Terry Gross, interview of Diana Henriques, "Examining Bernie Madoff, 'The Wizard of Lies,'" NPR, April 26, 2011, http://www.npr.org/templates/transcript/transcript.php?storyId=135706926.
9. James B. Stewart, *Tangled Webs: How False Statements Are Undermining America* (New York: Penguin Press, 2011).

10 https://www.youtube.com/watch?v=D7_dZTrjw9I.
11 See the Reverend Robert A. Gallagher's work on this. I borrow his thinking on this here. For a more comprehensive study, see his book *Fill All Things: The Dynamics of Spirituality in the Parish Church* (West Chester, PA: Ascension Press, 2008).
12 David Brooks, "The Humble Hound," *New York Times*, April 8, 2010, http://www.nytimes.com/2010/04/09/opinion/09brooks.html.
13 Ibid.
14 Ibid.
15 Ibid.
16 *The Rule of St. Benedict,* chapter 7.
17 Daniel B. Klein, "I Was Wrong, and So Are You," *The Atlantic,* December 2011, http://www.theatlantic.com/magazine/archive/2011/12/i-was-wrong-and-so-are-you/308713/.
18 BCP, 268.
19 Please see Jonathan Haidt's website for more information on this research: http://righteousmind.com.
20 www.valuebasedmanagement.net/methods_beckhard_change_model.html.
21 Jeffrey D. Jones, *Heart, Mind, and Strength: Theory and Practice for Congregational Leadership* (Herndon, VA: Alban Institute, 2009).
22 *The Godfather,* directed by Francis Ford Coppola (1972; Hollywood, CA: Paramount Home Video, 2001), DVD.
23 BCP, 305.

7

ASCETICAL COUNSEL FOR PARISH LEADERS

What follows comes from what I have learned along the way in the parishes I have lead, and now in the diocese I lead. I trust it will be good counsel. It comes from much grace and many bruises that I have received along the way.

Counsel as Clergy Begin in a New Parish

There is a natural, unavoidable process as new clergy arrive in parishes and begin their ministry with congregations. There are three stages: *Honeymoon*, *Disappointment*, and then, if the relationship has been able to endure through the first two stages, *Realistic Love and Reasonable Expectations*.[1] Let me explore each of these stages a bit from my own perspective and experience.

During the *Honeymoon*, as one might expect, everything is great. People love their new clergyperson. One might hear things like, "Their sermons are great. They're so personable and accessible." The clergyperson might be saying, "What great people. I'm so thankful to be here." But it is really a time of inflated and unreasonable expectations by everyone. As in a marriage, the honeymoon inevitably comes to an end. If it is falsely extended, then fantasy and self-delusion rule the day. It has to end so that a more realistic and mature relationship can be born in the future.

The next stage is *Disappointment*. It has a door that swings both ways as people learn their new clergyperson is not perfect. An incident occurs, or an interaction happens and they're disappointed. The spiritually mature will accept it because they know the clergyperson is human and will not always live up to their expectations, but the less spiritually mature will murmur, gripe, and gossip (often in the parking lot) about what is lacking in the new priest. The clergyperson also must face their own disappointment when they, in due course, realize the parish is not all they hoped, that the people are not everything they wanted them to be. It is a crucial time for all. If it can be navigated with perspective, grace, and forbearance, then the fruit produced in the future can be glorious.

The third stage is a time of *Realistic Love and Reasonable Expectations* when the parish comes to love the clergyperson for who they are, warts and all, and forms reasonable expectations for the leadership they bring. For the clergyperson, it is a time when they can fully accept the mixed bag their parishioners are and can love them as they are and not as they fantasize them to be. They can even love those less spiritually mature folks who cannot accept the priest's humanity, failures, and faults. It can be a time of great fruitfulness in the parish. Most often this stage happens sometime in the second or third year of a clergyperson's tenure (although it may be somewhat earlier or later), and it can last many years as long as together they remain focused on the spiritual practices of grace and forbearance.

Of course, sometimes clergy and people never make it to stage three. And occasionally, the stages can be quite short. I once had a honeymoon of about twenty minutes (the story I related in chapter four on the Promise of Obedience). If the clergy and people do not work together through the first two stages, they can get stuck, resentment can set in, and one or both can emotionally or spiritually check out, while physically staying in the parish. They must commit to work through the *Honeymoon* and *Disappointment* to reap the fruit of the shared love that will come.

Counsel on How to Deal with Parishioners' Fears

I explored this subject somewhat in chapter five when I wrote about human anxiety, but dealing with parishioners' fears needs its own counsel. Our human fears are often rational. When walking along a cliff face without a handrail or barrier, most of us experience fear. It is part of our human instinct for self-preservation. A lot of fear, however, is irrational: our anxieties are ginned up, or we are told to have anxieties by people who wish to manipulate us.

Recently there have been lawsuits in the British courts concerning churches that are seeking to replace their pews with chairs. Some parishioners sued the churchwardens to keep the chairs out and the pews in. As Sonny Corleone in *The Godfather* said, they were "going to the mattresses"[2] to keep the pews. Though not as prevalent, there are similar struggles on this side of the pond. One parish in the United States had to delay its building program for two years, not because they were underfunded or could not get a loan, but because the congregation was so deeply and emotionally divided over the choice between pews and chairs in the nave. They eventually went with the chairs. Nobody died, to my knowledge.

What is going on with this kind of reaction from people in churches? We could make sense of a parish struggle over which neighborhood it should evangelize or in which particular way they were going to serve the poor in their community or how they might use their property to be good neighbors to their community.

Those are worthy parish struggles. But pews vs. chairs? Really? It does seem petty. Is it worth paralyzing the parish so God's mission takes a back seat? Clearly, however, it is not petty to those in the fight. Something deeper is going on and the pews vs. chairs fight is just the presenting issue. We see similar paralysis elsewhere in the culture. Boards of education are unable to agree on textbooks for their students because of science being politicized; museum trustees are closing their institutions because they are unable to agree on which art to display; and members of Congress are shutting down the federal government when some of the members do not get their way.

People are reacting this way because they are fearful for reasons they might not even be able to articulate. The fear they are experiencing comes from a deep grief. It is a kind of death for them. And because grief is such a confusing, unpleasant, and difficult emotion for many people, rather than owning their grief, they manifest it outwardly as anger toward those proposing a change from what they are accustomed. From my experience, it does no good to tell fearful, grieving people to just get over it. That just makes them angrier. Nor does it do much good to tell them that their grieving is holding back the Church's mission. They simply get stuck deeper in their grief and fear and may cut off future dialogue. What has a chance to work for us is to take them and their grief seriously. Acknowledge that what they perceive as a loss matters to them. Then work toward a future that takes them and their concerns seriously. That does not mean, however, the pews will stay.

In a former parish, I had a parishioner at the annual parish meeting loudly scream against our proposed plans to redesign our worship space so it could be expanded to hold more, yes, chairs. I thought he was going to have a stroke. His anger seemed so disproportional. We did not halt the plans because he acted out, but we did listen to him (after he calmed down), tried to understand what he perceived he would be losing in the change, and asked him to help us work toward a redesign that would take his concerns seriously. He did not get everything he wanted in that redesign, but he had some good ideas that helped retain some of the previous effect of the worship space. We incorporated those ideas to everyone's delight. Most importantly, we honored a brother in Christ by taking him seriously. And he turned out to be the biggest giver in the fundraising effort that followed.

Counsel on Welcoming Guilt (It Can Be Good)

A recent study in the *Journal of Personality and Social Psychology* concluded that "guilt proneness is a critical characteristic of leaders."[3] The authors explained their findings by postulating that a sense of responsibility *for* others and *to* others explains why effective leaders are more guilt-prone than less effective leaders. This makes sense for parish leaders. If we see ourselves as mistake free, or unburdened about being wrong, or incapable of recognizing our complicity when things fall apart, then we are not going to be very effective leaders, especially in the church. A crucial part of being faithful, effective leaders means that we will not only have empathy for others when they fail, but we will also have a real sense of responsibility—and yes, guilt—when we ourselves fail. The former lets those we lead know we have solidarity with them from our own experience and the latter keeps us from thinking, as St. Paul wrote, "of yourself more highly than you ought to think" (Rom. 12:3).

Of course, there are people who suffer inappropriately from guilt. In those situations, their guilt is disordered. They are ready to admit to crimes and misdemeanors they did not even commit. Guilt can be paralyzing for these people, but that is a small percentage. It is important for us to have a healthy, spiritually grounded appreciation for, and personal acceptance of, our own faults and failures and the resulting guilt that comes from such an acknowledgment. Being truthful will surely leave us vulnerable and open to attack, give those opposed to our leadership fuel to criticize us, and, among the spiritually immature, leave them convinced we are less than we should be (that should not be a newsflash to any Christian). So be it. The alternative is worse. It means buying into the sociopathology of our culture.

Counsel on Getting the Parish Unstuck from Learned Helplessness

In his book *Simply Effective: How to Cut Through Complexity in Your Organization and Get Things Done*,[4] Ron Ashkenas says many organizations develop what he calls *learned helplessness* over time, as leaders in an organization slowly create a list of excuses and explanations for why the organization cannot change or improve as it seeks to accomplish its mission. Ashkenas says that rather than finding ways to make things better, or generating ideas for how things might be different, leaders instead gradually accept the status quo and use external forces to explain and then to excuse the "stuckness" of the organization.

Learned helplessness can become viral in any organization, and the church is no exception. In congregations, I hear regularly language that says, "We're stuck." What often follows is their reason for being stuck. It rarely is their fault:

"If the national Church would just stop taking liberal positions on things, then we'd be fine."

"There just aren't that many Episcopalians moving into our town these days."

"We just don't have enough money or people to get anything done. If we had more of both, then we'd be fine."

I often reply to this last excuse by asking how much it actually costs to love our neighbor as ourselves? These examples are just excuses for congregations to do little to proclaim the gospel in their communities. By treating themselves as victims of the larger Church's actions, dwindling populations, or the lack of resources, they display a sense of learned helplessness in its clearest form.

Ashkenas offers a way to get beyond learned helplessness. He says organizations should name clearly what is going on. He suggests making a list of initiatives people say they want but have not done, followed by a list of the ten most common excuses for why there has been inaction. Creating dialogue helps everyone become aware of their complicity in learned helplessness.

In the church, we hear, "We don't have enough people. We don't have enough resources. We don't have enough time. We tried something new before and it didn't work." Following Ashkenas's directions, what if a parish found just one initiative that could show even in a small way that the organization can accomplish something? In congregations where people have adopted the passive resignation of learned helplessness, too often they think they need large, bold initiatives, which has the tendency to scare people and make them even less likely to become unstuck. What works is to find one simple thing that the parish can do together that is likely achievable, and then to do it. Once it is achieved, celebrate the success. In one of my former parishes, we wanted to grow the Sunday school. We had one child and when we got a second, we celebrated that Sunday school attendance had doubled in just one week. If congregations can take that first small step to become unstuck, then they can celebrate their way to the next.

Counsel on Changing the Parish's Emotional Climate

One of the recurring laments I hear from parish leaders is their perception that many of their parishioners do not have a serious investment in the church's mission. They are not saying laity lack a love for God, or that they do not desire for the parish to flourish, but the leadership's experience is that the laity are not committed enough to the transformation of their church into a vital center of mission for Jesus Christ. While there may be a few laity out there who truly fit that definition, my experience tells me that the problem is not a lack of commitment from the laity; rather it is a lack of emotionally intelligent leadership.

In their book *The Progress Principle: Using Small Wins to Ignite Joy, Engagement, and Creativity at Work*,[5] Teresa Amabile and Steven Kramer describe a widespread problem they found in many of the businesses and organizations they studied. Leaders regularly and unconsciously inhibit the commitment and creativity of the people with whom they work, which ultimately hurts the emotional inner lives of employees because they lose their personal engagement and connectivity with their work. The authors conclude that it is an avoidable dynamic. They argue that employees both want and need to make real progress toward meaningful work. They write about the "inner work life" of employees. When this inner work life is attended to, even in small ways, employees become more creative, productive, committed, and collegial in their jobs. Before setting production metrics, work goals, or strategic objectives, leaders would do well to focus on creating the conditions for their employees to develop positive inner work lives. For things to be positive for the long haul, employees must actually experience—in tangible ways—some personal meaning in their work. When they do, their commitment to and investment in the goals of the organization deepen and become widely shared.

This research speaks to how we can lead more effectively in the church. We often wrongly assess laity as being complacent, or apathetic, or lacking sufficient motivation to accomplish the goals of the church's mission, when what might be going on is that we have failed to engage their inner spiritual lives in such a way that connects their personal spiritual practices with the larger mission of the church. Without attending seriously to the inner spiritual lives of the laity, we unconsciously inhibit their commitment and, consequently, their creativity and passion for the church's mission. We ought to spend less time on grand strategies and audacious goals. They are important in the long run, but they are the cart before the horse, so to speak. The laity first must be helped to attend to their inner spiritual lives through meaningful personal spiritual practices that are grounded in our tradition,[6] which will help them develop an inside-out commitment to the gospel and leave us with no reason to lament their lack of commitment. We will actually find ourselves leading a congregation alive with missionary zeal.

Counsel on Refocusing the Parish

Parish leaders can have enormous impact on the health and vitality of the congregations they lead. But often the day-to-day running of the parish gets so much of our attention that we have little time or energy to work on the practices that lead to such health and vitality. The urgent triumphs over the important. Grounding people in the traditional spiritual practices of the Church must be our primary task. If that grounding is not present in the congregation, then it is time to refocus. Rather than us focusing on running the parish, we must place most of our energies on grounding people in the faith and practice of the Church, growing the leadership base of the congregation, and creating a disciplined listening process for what God is up to in our midst. Here is what that could look like:[7]

1. Hold a recurring class that cycles about every six to eight weeks. The class would teach people how to engage in the spiritual practices of the Church. Sessions ought to include: what is the Great Narrative of Redemption, how do we pray the Daily Office, what does sacramental living look like, how do we keep Sabbath time, what does being a steward of God's blessings mean, and where can we exercise our Christian service in the world? The class builds up the basic skills of the laity's discipleship. Over time, it develops a critical mass of lay leaders who are mature in their faith.

2. Regularly meet with existing leaders to identify future leaders and then nurture those folks. Done right, this does not threaten current leaders, especially if you enlist them as mentors for future leaders. Congregations who

are constantly developing leaders and equipping them to be good at what they do will always have people in place who have the energy and the smarts to lead.

3. Have open meetings twice a year, in addition to the annual meeting of the parish. They need to be well planned and designed to draw feedback from people on how the congregation is doing; where people can share their hopes, raise concerns, and offer their thoughts on ways to make things better. It is human nature to want to be heard. Often, brewing low-grade conflicts can be addressed before they get larger simply by respectful listening and clear response. It also has the benefit for leaders in that they get to see where the energy is in the congregation. What ideas or hopes seem to have the most enthusiasm? Go with those. If there is no energy around the annual (fill in the blank), then let it go for now. Trying to create energy where is none will not produce anything good in the short run. It will merely exhaust the parish leadership before any healthy movement has begun.

Counsel on the *Askesis* of Forgiveness

Askesis is the work we do to be bearers and stewards of the Great Narrative of Redemption. *Askeses* are not about the values we hold. Values are changeable because they represent commitments we hold in relationship to other commitments. For example, we might say we value time with our family more than we value time at work. Values have a price tag on them and we daily weigh the cost of holding one value in relationship to another. *Askeses*, the practices Christians engage in as disciples of Jesus, however, are ways of being we hold to be immutable. *Askeses,* like truthfulness, compassion, and mercy, cannot be values we hold. They are ways of being and acting in the world. We cannot value compassion. We either live compassionately or we do not. Christianity is less a set of beliefs we hold, rather the *askeses* we embody. The creeds of the Church are not set before us so we can be challenged to believe them. Rather, they are a summary of the faith Christians have practiced for millennia.

In Galatians 5, St. Paul writes, "The fruit of the Spirit is love, joy, peace, patience, kindness, generosity, faithfulness, gentleness, and self-control. There is no law against such things" (verses 22–23). He is listing the *askeses* we are to incarnate in our lives. When he writes, "There is no law against such things," he acknowledges that these are practices that cannot be commanded, but ways of being that disciples cultivate in their lives. Such cultivation of *askeses* is a lifelong discipline for all disciples of Jesus, us included.

Probably the most challenging of all the Christian practices is forgiveness. It is also the practice Jesus addresses most often. He makes it a central part of what we now call The Lord's Prayer ("Forgive us our sins, for we ourselves forgive everyone indebted to us" [Luke 11:4]). Jesus clearly saw forgiveness as being the lever that enabled all other practices. Without the capacity to forgive, incarnating other practices simply is not possible. Yet, forgiving others is hard work for us to practice. The hurt can be so deep. The desire for vengeance can be so powerful. We must remember this is not a minor teaching by Jesus, or one that can be open to several interpretations. Jesus is clear: we must forgive.

The Church teaches us much about forgiveness. She teaches us that our primary identity is as a child of God. Such an identity cannot be lost in our interaction with others, even if others sin against us, or if we sin against them. That is why Jesus calls us to seek reconciliation:

> When you are offering your gift at the altar, if you remember that your brother or sister has something against you, leave your gift there before the altar and go; first be reconciled to your brother or sister, and then come and offer your gift. (Matt. 5:23–24)

Jesus knows that our lack of forgiveness prevents us from finding our identity in a God whose very nature is forgiveness. Our call is to practice forgiveness as the central *askesis* of our Christian faith.

David Brooks, a columnist for the *New York Times*, wrote:

> James McNulty had a paper in the *Journal of Family Psychology* last year suggesting that forgiveness has a down side. It may increase the chances that those who are forgiven will offend again. McNulty studied family diaries and found that newlywed partners were more likely to report misbehavior on days after they were forgiven for something else. It should be added that forgiveness is still a good thing to do. The downside probably doesn't outweigh the positive effects.[8]

I have enormous respect for David Brooks, but I find what he wrote somewhat humorous—an indication that he apparently has a pretty paltry understanding of forgiveness. The humorous aspect is simply the human condition. If we do not find human behavior in all its complexities somewhat humorous, we are not paying attention to ourselves or to the people around us. Of course, an immature reaction to being forgiven is to see it as an apparent license to misbehave again. Human beings do such silly, immature things. But I would argue that the person who does so repeatedly does not fully comprehend love or the depths of what forgiveness means. That is the paltry side.

Forgiveness, as it is lived in Christian discipleship, becomes unintelligible if we first weigh its downside or upside before forgiving. If we stop to calculate its positive or negative effects, we miss the whole point of why Jesus makes it plain that forgiveness is at the heart of the gospel. We do not forgive because it works, or because it has a greater upside than downside. We forgive, quite simply, because it is the way God has given us to share in the very life of God. Whether or not the other person is remorseful is beside the point. We can hold that hope, but it is not a necessary condition for forgiveness. Practicing forgiveness is about us, not the transgressor. It is about our relationship with God. Yes, other people can hurt us deeply. And, yes, that hurt can be so painful it lasts for years. Yet, Jesus takes all the subjectivity out of it when he very clearly commands us to forgive one another.

I am not making light of the pain we suffer as a result of another person's sin against us. Sometimes it feels bone-shattering. I am certainly not suggesting that forgiveness is easy or quickly accomplished. Often it is a process that takes a very long time. Still, it is central to our identity as disciples of Jesus and to our practice of the Christian faith. As St. Paul writes in Romans 5:8, "While we were yet sinners, Christ died for us." God did not take a Gallup poll to see if we would be remorseful or thankful that Jesus died for us. God just did it. It is God's nature. It is who God is in Jesus Christ without qualification or condition.

Counsel on Humility in Parish Leadership

> I . . . have the impression that God knows the importance of humility for man. He knows our weakness, our pride, and . . . He purposely sets in our path each day four or five humiliations, and in the course of our life, four or five great humiliations. If we do not comprehend them, if we do not accept them, it is a serious matter. But if we accept them, then we learn the generosity of God.[9]
>
> —Dom Helder Camara

Ministry is humbling. Done right, as St. Paul implies, we will exercise such ministry as "fools for Christ's sake." In an increasingly post-Christian context, what we do in the name of Christ as ministers of his gospel will look more and more like foolishness to others. Given the current wisdom of the world, what could be more foolish than proclaiming, "Christ has died, Christ is risen, Christ will come again"? Such foolishness leads us, by intention or not, to the occasional humiliation—at least by human standards. We, of course, should not seek out such humiliation. We should not be gluttons for punishment. As Archbishop Tutu is fond of saying, "The meek are called to inherit the earth, not eat the dirt." When we do experience humiliation in our ministries, we should not wear it as a badge of honor, showing others what a dedicated martyr we are to the cause of Christ. That is seeking humility in the wrong way. Even as we minister, striving to be faithful and effective, we will fail, and sometimes extraordinarily so. From it, we hopefully will learn and not repeat those same failures again (do not worry, there will be new ones to experience). Our failures should never be ignored or unexamined. We should not forget them. In remembering them, we experience God's forgiveness, and even may learn to forgive ourselves. In these times of humiliation, as Helder Camara suggests above, "We learn the generosity of God."

I recently had an experience where I was humiliated by my actions. No one else realized it, but I did. After I finished mentally and spiritually kicking myself over an extended period of time for what I had done, I asked God's forgiveness. I learned something about myself in that humiliation. Whenever I find myself in a similar context again, I am confident I will remind myself of what went before. Our memory is also part of God's generosity. It can help us grow into the full stature of Christ.

The issue is not how we can insulate ourselves from potential humiliation. Leadership requires vulnerability. Otherwise, we would never risk anything for the sake of the gospel. No, the issue is: Do we have a spiritual inbox? Are we open to learning more about ourselves and our ministry? Are we willing to do the hard work of self-examination and growth that can come when we are brought low and humiliated by our actions? The Church desperately needs leaders who are so inclined.

Counsel on Modeling Repentance in the Parish

Repentance is at the heart of welcoming Christ into our lives that he might shape and rule our hearts. When parishioners see us engaging in it on a regular basis, it invites them (or gives them permission) to do so themselves. Repentance, biblically speaking, means to change one's understanding (*metanoia* = *meta*—change, and *noia*—understanding) in light of the Great Narrative of Redemption. We can invite parishioners into this *askesis* by our own openness to repentance. Parishioners must see repentance in us in order to know what it looks like. Our openness will create a certain amount of vulnerability, as I wrote in chapter five on the Promise of Conversion of Life. So be it. It is worth the risk. Our witness in our *askesis* of repentance will have a *conversio* effect on the spiritual climate of the parish.

My own experience of repentance tells me that it is life-altering for me personally and for my leadership in the church. My repentance has caused me to place less importance on the ways I have defined differences in people with whom I serve in the church. It has helped me see them as sacred creations whom Jesus came to save and set free. It has brought me to a point where I care less about being right and more about doing right. I find myself caring less about differences of opinion between myself and other people in the church and more about what I and other people do with our lives. The more I practice repentance now, the less I care about someone's political affiliation and the more I care about the fruit produced by that person's life. The more I practice repentance in my own life, the more I try to see the world from God's perspective found in Jesus, which means I am less worried about the fate of the earth. That is not to say I have adopted a Pollyannaish worldview. Just because we try to see the world as God sees it doesn't mean we need to be in denial about the world's reality. God, of course, has never been in denial about Creation. The Cross of Jesus is God's declarative statement that God has accepted the world as it is, and the Resurrection of Jesus is God's clear statement that the world (as it is) is unacceptable to God. The Cross and Resurrection help us all keep God's big picture in mind. If we have come to believe the world is a vicious, unforgiving, meaningless place, that simply means we have not yet repented. Our repentance changes the way we see the world. For us, that is crucial.

Counsel on Resisting Flattery from Parishioners

In the spring 2011 issue of *The Hedgehog Review*, Thomas de Zengotita writes about what he calls "the flattery of representation."[10] He writes:

> We have been consigned by it to a new plane of being, a new kind of life-world, an environment of representations of fabulous quality and inescapable ubiquity, a place where everything is addressed to us, everything is for us, and nothing is beyond us anymore.[11]

Zengotita contends that ubiquitous media flatter us with attention. We get our own personal mobile ringtones and our choice of individualized media when we go online.

In this age, life is designed to focus *on us* and *for us*. As social media leads to social movements like MoveOn or the Tea Party, they thrive because they create the illusion that each participant is indispensably at the center of the movement. The reality, of course, is different. Each participant is actually being manipulated to accomplish a particular group's agenda. Is it any wonder then we have the current political climate? Each legislator is saturated by media flattery, so why would they not expect to get exactly what they want with no need to listen to another's point of view or to consider compromise? Why compromise when we believe the world really should be our oyster?

Media and particularly advertisers have always known that flattery sells. An Oldsmobile ad a few years ago promised that when you turned your Oldsmobile on, it would then "turn you on." A Reebok ad promised that if you wore their sneakers, then it would let "you be you." Even the U.S. Army decided it needed to flatter to bump up enlistment, so they promised that you could be an "Army of One," or, if you joined, you could "be all that you can be." (My hunch is the drill instructors at boot camp did not confirm that.) Flattery for the sake of manipulation has been with us for a long time. What is different now is that such flattery is hyper-realized with so many more media inputs in our lives, all of which flatter the inner narcissist in us all.

If Zengotita is observing our present age accurately, then the Church—particularly the leadership—has an enormous challenge in terms of communicating the Great Narrative of Redemption, for it is fundamentally not about us. It is for us, but not about us. It tells us we are not the principal actors on the world's stage. We are, at best, bit players in the narrative God is unfolding. The world is not about our desires and preferences. It is about what God has done and is doing in the Great Narrative. That is a tough sell to people who have come to believe life should only really be about what they want. In a world where everyone is special and demands to be catered to, the gospel must seem a foreign language. As some churches have learned, you can always draw a crowd when you flatter and entertain your audience (see: Osteen, Joel) and refrain from telling them that the Gospel of Jesus makes demands upon their lives. There is always a market in the Church for snake oil versions of the gospel. H. Richard Niebuhr described this snake oil gospel this way: "A God without wrath brought men without sin into a kingdom without judgment through the ministrations of a Christ without a cross."[12]

This is the larger context in which we live and lead. We can fall victim to the flattering voice just as easily as anyone else. Our vocation is so impossibly hard and we often go underappreciated, so when we do hear the voice of flattery, we may not be able to distinguish it from a compliment. Sometimes it is impossible because we cannot know the motives of the person speaking. My counsel is to play it safe. We should of course listen to all the good press we receive, but hold it loosely. When I receive such talk, I remember to share it with my spiritual director. She has a way of helping me sift through the differences between flattery and compliments.

Counsel on Learning from Failure in the Parish

In his book *Adapt: Why Success Always Starts with Failure*, Tim Harford brings the disciplines of psychology, evolutionary biology, anthropology, physics, and economics together to make a profoundly simple argument: life cannot be lived well if all we seek are easy solutions or even expert opinions. Our world is far too chaotic and complex for such facile approaches or an overreliance on ivory tower pronouncements. Harford rather contends it is all about how we adapt and respond to our failures through trial and error. His basic lesson is: we have to design into our efforts to make effective use of our failures; we have to design our life's efforts to make use of trial and error. Most efforts, he argues, succeed by stumbling and adapting, not by meticulous planning or grand schemes. He lays out a three-point process:

1. Discover new ideas and new ways of doing things;
2. try them on a small scale so if you fail you can survive the consequences; and
3. establish a feedback loop so you can find out what is failing and what is working.

He argues this process works in almost all contexts, from business to war to writing. Hartford is an economist, so he is not writing about the *askeses* of parish leadership, but if we translate some of his terms into our language of faith, then he describes a useful road map for those of us who are trying to lead faithfully. As we seek to lead, particularly as we work to reach new people with the gospel, his approach is right on target. We have to be willing to try new approaches that we have not tried before. And we will have to be open to failure in those efforts, because some of them will fail. As Harford reminds us, failure is not the problem. The issue is not learning from our failure through a feedback loop.

Like everyone else, we find comfort in the familiar and in what we have done before. We are just as hesitant to opening ourselves up to trial, error, and adaptation as our congregations are. We are just as likely to say, "I never do things that way," or "I tried something similar ten years ago and it didn't work." What if we are willing to try new approaches, learning from how previous ones did not work, and then trying new variations on our successful efforts? The content of the Church's Great Narrative of Redemption is elegantly true and without flaw. It is our approach to sharing the message that needs constant scrutiny and a willingness to adapt as we learn from our mistakes.

Counsel on Truthfulness: Come What May, Cost What It Will

> Daily prayers and religious reading and church-going are necessary parts of the Christian life. We have to be continually reminded of what we believe.
> —C. S. Lewis, *Mere Christianity*

C. S. Lewis, as with most of his observations about God and human nature, is right on target. We do "have to be continually reminded of what we believe" because we human beings are not nearly as smart as we would hope. It is necessary for us to have the daily reinforcement of Jesus's teachings in the Gospels, what the Church proclaims to be true in the creeds, and the common prayer of the saints on earth and in heaven. Without such regular reintegration of the faith, we may not forget entirely who we are in Christ, but we may get distracted or even deceived (see John 10).

Those who wish to influence us and other members of the public are counting on our vulnerability to distraction and deception. A few years ago, Senator Jon Kyl said, "If you want an abortion, you go to Planned Parenthood, and that's well over 90 percent of what Planned Parenthood does." A fact-check of the services of Planned Parenthood determined that only 3 percent of their services are abortion related. Later his staff issued a clarification stating the senator's remark "was not intended to be a factual statement but rather to illustrate that Planned Parenthood, an organization that receives millions in taxpayer dollars, does subsidize abortions." If it was not intended to be a factual statement, then why did he say it? I share Senator Kyl's uneasiness about abortion, but facts cannot be made up. Mark Twain famously said, "There are three kinds of lies: lies, damned lies, and statistics."[13]

Senator Kyl is by no means alone and it is almost unfair to single him out because lying is becoming commonplace. Public figures of all persuasions are making up facts to suit themselves. Visit the Pulitzer Prize–winning organization *Politifact*, and you can see that Senator Kyl is in good, or bad, company as the case may be. Many people seem to have adopted Stephen Colbert's satirical standard of truth, which he has called "truthiness." He defines it as something that sounds true to the hearer so it must be true. A new postmodern paradigm has arrived that proclaims truth as whatever someone says passionately enough and whatever enough people want to believe. For example, just because some people do not want to believe that human activity is contributing significantly to climate change, which is disastrous for the earth, does not mean it is not true. The overwhelming scientific evidence says climate change is a reality.

Truth, however, cannot be so mutable and pliable that it can be changed or bent to our will and desires. Truth exists beyond our biases and prejudices. That is the danger embedded in our present cultural ethos around truth. Many people are playing fast and loose with the truth and that might lead people to accept such practice as normative. "Everyone does it" will become a common justification. Where will such a stance toward truth leave us as a people?

This is the last of my ascetical counsel because I believe it is the most important of all. We must be people who are committed to "seek the truth, come what may, cost what it will."[14] Stephen Colbert's truthiness will not do. In our present culture, truth-telling is in short supply. We must be bold enough to speak the truth regardless of the consequences. And we must be humble enough to accept the consequences when they come, because they always do. My experience has shown me that the truth will always prevail, even if it prevails in ways we do not understand. At the end of our parish ministries, we may not have a whole lot to show for ourselves. We may not have built up large congregations or have been known as great preachers. But is there any reason we could not be known for our truth-telling? The Great Narrative of Redemption on which we have staked our lives demands we speak the truth, first to ourselves and then to the people God has given us to lead. That is why God called us to this impossible vocation. It is the least we can do.

NOTES

1 I draw here on the work of the Reverend Robert A. Gallagher, OA, in his *Bonding of Priest and Community*. A pdf of his thinking is found at: http://static1.1.sqspcdn.com/static/f/1002566/25440987/1410746714937/Bonding+Priest+and+Community.pdf?token=IvAYRqjMTDfoAWNkRFtwzUD0PgE%3D.

2 *The Godfather*, directed by Francis Ford Coppola (1972; Hollywood, CA: Paramount Home Video, 2001), DVD.

3 Rebecca L. Schaumberg and Francis J. Flynn, "Uneasy Lies the Head That Wears the Crown: The Link between Guilt-Proneness and Leadership," *Journal of Personality and Social Psychology* 103, issue 2 (August 2012): 327–42.

4 I read an overview of his book and thinking on this subject at the *Harvard Business Review*: https://hbr.org/product/simply-effective-how-to-cut-through-complexity-in-/an/10037-HBK-ENG.

5 Teresa Amabile and Steven Kramer, *The Progress Principle: Using Small Wins to Ignite Joy, Engagement, and Creativity at Work* (Grand Haven, MI: Brilliance Audio, 2014), Audio CD.
6 See Michelle Heyne, OA, in her book, *In Your Holy Spirit: Traditional Spiritual Practices in Today's Christian Life* (West Chester, PA: Ascension Press, 2011).
7 These are based on numerous conversations I have had with the Reverend Robert A. Gallagher, OA, over the years on this topic.
8 David Brooks, "Forgiveness," *New York Times*, March 9, 2011, http://brooks.blogs.nytimes.com/2011/03/09/forgiveness/.
9 Quoted in the Rule of the Order of the Ascension, http://static1.1.sqspcdn.com/static/f/1124858/26280250/1433264322093/The+Rule+of+the+Order+of+the+Ascension+as+of+May+2015.pdf?token=2syc7l4RPN0W4ul47hBWovCaDZY%3D.
10 Thomas de Zengotita, "On the Politics of Pastiche and Depthless Intensities: The Case of Barack Obama," *The Hedgehog Review* 13, no. 1 (spring 2011), http://www.iasc-culture.org/THR/THR_article_2011_Spring_Zengotita.php.
11 Ibid.
12 H. Richard Niebuhr, *The Kingdom of God in America* (New York: Harper & Row, 1959), 193.
13 The quote has been attributed to Mark Twain, but its actual source is unknown.
14 This is a quote from advice that the Reverend William Sparrow gave to his students at the Virginia Theological Seminary. Sparrow taught history, theology, and Christian evidences at the seminary from 1841 until his death in 1874.

CONCLUSION
(OR, HOW THIS MIGHT
MAKE SENSE AND WORK)

What I have offered in these pages will serve us well only if it works as a stance and approach to ministry that is also accompanied by a set of practices (*askeses*) that help us survive and thrive. In a sense, what I have presented is a Rule of Life, or *Regula*, for church leaders. Like with the Rule of St. Benedict, or any other rule, it must make sense, and be manageable and realistic, based on who we are and the context in which we live. And it must practically work for us or it is useless. A Rule of Life, however, must be more than manageable, realistic, and practical. It also must call us to something beyond ourselves, something sacrificial and holy, that responds faithfully to the claims of Christ on our lives.

What I have proposed in these chapters are various *askeses* that, when practiced, hopefully will lead us to what Aristotle called *eudaemonia (eudaimonia)*, which literally means a "well-spirit" (*eu* = well and *daimon* = spirit). *Eudaemonia*, however, has often been translated as "happiness," which I believe wrongly connotes what Aristotle intended. He did not understand *eudaemonia* as mere happiness. That English word seems too superficial and does not do it justice. Aristotle was describing what I would rather call a "soul wellness"[1] that comes from living out certain virtues he defined.

So, for the Christian, we might say that *eudaemonia* comes as a result of living out *askeses* congruent with our baptismal identity and purpose. For clergy leaders, this means *askeses* that are true to our ordination vows to serve God in that "wonderful and sacred mystery" of the Church. These *askeses*, however, will become another avenue that leads us to creep toward works righteousness if they do not proceed out of a deep reliance on God's grace. The best stance, the wisest approach, or the strongest *askeses* will not save us. Only God's grace in Jesus will do that.

In the powerful film *Tender Mercies*, Robert Duvall plays a washed-up, alcoholic country singer named Mac Sledge who finds recovery and redemption through his newfound sobriety, marriage to a widow (played by Tess Harper), and his adoption of her young son as his own. Toward the end of the film, Mac is silently working in the family garden behind their house. Much has happened since his sobriety and marriage, including the tragic car accident and death of his eighteen-year-old daughter from his previous marriage. As he is working in the garden, trying to understand his grief, Harper's character comes out to check on him and asks him how he is doing. He tells her he does not understand why everything has happened. By all rights, he should have been dead due to the reckless and self-centered life he has lived. And yet, he is alive and his daughter is dead. He does not understand why his life is now redeemed and whole. Somehow, things are not right. He finishes their garden interaction by saying to his wife, "You see, I don't trust happiness. I never did. I never will."[2]

To me, those are the most powerful words in a film full of amazing writing because Mac Sledge, even in his overwhelming grief, has a soul wellness beyond and more vital than what might be called happiness. He has received grace upon grace from his new wife, his adopted son, and the new friends he has made. The film ends with the *askesis* of Mac tossing a football back and forth with his adopted son. The look on Mac's face says it all. His grief is not gone. His past is not forgotten. But there is a soul wellness with him as the football goes back and forth.

It is such soul wellness that I am still learning how to receive through God's grace and then by practicing it. I long for my fellow clergy to learn and practice this as well. We will not reach soul wellness, however, through the pursuit of happiness. Such a pursuit is part of the American narrative and myth that has to some degree shaped us all. Thomas Jefferson wrote the following to a friend in 1763:

> Perfect happiness I believe was never intended by the deity to be the lot of any one of his creatures in this world; but that he has very much put in our power the nearness of our approaches to it, is what I as steadfastly believe.[3]

Jefferson thought that if we just worked hard enough at it, we had the power to get near to perfect happiness, or at least to doggedly pursue it. That pursuit has become a central part of our cultural mythos. It has been deeply ingrained in us from our beginning. It has been and continues to serve as a form of the law about which St. Paul wrote.[4] It has become a Kantian categorical imperative for us and, when we fail to achieve it—and we always will—we judge ourselves harshly as we receive the judgment of others for our failure. Happiness, therefore, becomes something we must pursue like everything else. It becomes a measurable contest to see who can get the most of it. Soul wellness for Christians, however, is not achieved by pursuing happiness. It is reached through resting in the grace of God as we live into our identity and purpose in Christ. His gospel makes it clear that through resting in God's tender mercies we will find meaning in our lives and our true destiny as the children of God.

The Science of Happiness

In the behavioral sciences, researchers who study happiness have begun to change their conclusions about what happiness constitutes and even if it is necessary for a well-lived life. They, too, have learned not to see happiness as an end in itself. They are finding it is the sum of a person's sense of identity and purpose that produces soul wellness rather than the pursuit of happiness itself.

Discoveries in the field of social genomics seem to bear this out. Will Storr, writing in *The New Yorker*, reports on research that connects such soul wellness with human flourishing.[5] By taking blood samples from a variety of test subjects after they have been thoroughly interviewed about their lives, they found a connection between Aristotle's *eudaemonia*, his soul wellness, and people's general health and vitality. In fact, lacking such *eudaemonia* "can be as damaging as smoking or obesity."[6] Those whose blood work showed the most genomic health were those who had a purpose in life that coincided with their identity. It has led the researchers to conclude that *eudaemonia* is not a feeling, but a practice, what I have called *askesis*. "It's living in a way that fulfills our purpose," Helen Morales, a classicist at the University of California, Santa Barbara, said. "Happiness is being engaged in the process." She used the Olympic sprinter Usain Bolt as an example. For him, "some of the training it takes to be a great athlete is not pleasurable, but fulfilling your purpose as a great runner brings happiness."[7]

To be sure, some of the training (*askesis*) an athlete endures is not fun. In my youth, I remember the three-a-day August practices preparing for football season. Likewise, in parish ministry, some of what we must practice is not always pleasurable. If, however, we are grounded in God's grace made possible through the Great Narrative of Redemption, and if we engage in the *askeses* that we have learned will work for us, then soul wellness can, and most likely will, be the result.

And Yet

We will still be broken by parish ministry. I would be lying to you in these pages if I did not write that clearly. God's grace and sound *askeses* are not prophylactics against being broken by this vocation. It will break the best of us. Any person who would willingly accept a call to ordained leadership in the church should rightly be suspect. They, as the saying goes, ought to have their heads examined, which of course is exactly what we do to candidates for ordination. The church puts her candidates through rigorous sets of psychological examinations. Then we only ordain those who are found to have significant enough psychological health. Maybe we are making a mistake? Maybe we should only ordain those who are, as my mother used to say, "crazier than a June bug"? After all, St. Paul tells us in the first chapter of 1 Corinthians that if we want to be disciples of Jesus and live into the Great Narrative of Redemption, then we'll appear to the rest of the world as nothing more than fools. As usual, St. Paul is right.

One of my mentors who helped shape me and lead me into ordained ministry was a Methodist pastor named Tex Evans. Tex described himself as "the biggest liar to ever come out of East Texas." He could weave a tall tale and tell some big lies (always with a twinkle in his eyes to let you know you were in on the joke with him). Tex worked among the poor of Appalachia for his entire ministry. In the late sixties, he had an epiphany. He saw all the horrible poverty among his people at the Redbird Mission in eastern Kentucky. He also knew there were church youth groups across the country that were full of idealism and a desire to help. Tex proposed bringing them together. His vision was to bring the youth groups to Appalachia so they could fix up and repair people's homes. The groups would pay for this privilege and they'd receive a crash course in the culture and economics of poverty. To make his idea work, he needed a base of operations. So, he asked the board of trustees of tiny Union College in eastern Kentucky to let him use their facilities to house the youth groups over the summer. The board listened to his plan and then asked him to wait outside while they deliberated. An hour later, the president of the college came out and said, "Pastor Evans, the board talked about this for a long time. We concluded this whole thing was just a bunch of foolishness; that only a fool would do such a thing. And, Pastor Evans, we think you're just the fool to do it!"[8]

Frederick Buechner, speaking to a seminary graduating class, made a similar case for the foolishness of ministry, particularly parish ministry:

> It's a queer business that you have chosen or that has chosen you. It's a business that breaks the heart for the sake of the heart. It's a hard and chancy business whose risks are as great even as its rewards. Above all else, perhaps, it is a crazy business. It is a foolish business. It is a crazy and foolish business to work for Christ in a world where most people most of the time don't give a hoot in hell whether you work for him or not. It is crazy and foolish to offer a service that most people most of the time think they need like a hole in the head. As long as there are bones to set and drains to unclog and children to tame and boredom to survive, we need doctors and plumbers and teachers and people who play the musical saw; but when it comes to the business of Christ and his church, how unreal and irrelevant a service that seems even, and at times especially, to the ones who are called to work at it.[9]

But we are the kind of fools God uses to reconcile the world to God's self. Whenever the Church calls someone to ordained ministry, the Church is making both a proclamation and a protest, proclaiming that all people are called to follow Jesus and that some are called to follow him as ordained ministers. The church is also protesting against all ideologies and political systems that deny, distract, or dissuade people from their promised destiny in God.

In ordination, we take the heart of Jesus to the world. Our call is to tell the story of Jesus, to tell it truthfully, to tell it rightly, so that the Church can be a community where the story of Jesus is told and told truthfully and rightfully. The more we hear his story, the more we are both comforted and challenged. Jesus comforts us with his unmerited grace even as he challenges us to an impossible vocation. That is why ministry is always a fool's errand.

Every Lent I read *A Canticle for Leibowitz* by Walter Miller. It's about a postapocalyptic Christian monastic order: the Order of Leibowitz. At the end of the book, the monastery's old abbot is nearing death and a new one needs to be chosen.

> A young monk is put forward, but he's scared. He says to the abbot, "Father, I'm not certain. What will this mean?"
>
> The old abbot replies: "It means you'll be asked to be the ass on which Jesus rides into Jerusalem. It's a heavy load and it'll break your back, because He's carrying the sins of the world."
>
> The young monk replies: "Then I don't think I'm able."
>
> The old abbot answers: "Able? None of us has been able. But we've tried, and we've been tried. It tries you to destruction, but you're here for that. This Order has had abbots of gold, abbots of cold steel, abbots of corroded lead, and none of them was able. The gold got battered, the steel got brittle and broke, and the corroded lead got stamped into ashes. Me? I've been lucky enough to be quicksilver; I spatter, but I run back together somehow."
>
> "But Father I'm scared," the young monk answers.

The abbot replies: "Steel screams when it's forged, my boy, it gasps when it's quenched. It creaks when it goes under load. I think even steel is scared. If it makes you terrified, then scream. If it makes you anything, then pray. But come into church before Mass and tell me your answer."

Right before mass begins, the young monk comes to the old abbot and says: "If they choose me, I accept the honor."

The abbot smiles and says: "You heard me badly. I said burden not honor. Are you still certain?"

The young monk replies: "If they choose me, I shall be certain."[10]

I Leave You with This

Leading the church is indeed a burden, not an honor, but it is a burden we can bear well and effectively, even enjoy, if our trust is rooted in the grace of God and if our *askeses* shape our stance and approach to ministry in the rootedness of that grace. We can have soul wellness and thrive in the ministry to which we have been called. Soul wellness in ministry, however, means being hospitable first to ourselves and then to our family and others around us. Such hospitality means giving ourselves and others a break, showing ourselves and them grace and mercy, recognizing in ourselves and in them our common HPTFTU ("human propensity to f**k things up"). It means not taking ourselves and everything (other than God's grace) so seriously. The Greek New Testament word for hospitality is *philoxenia*, which literally means "to love strangers." It is the exact opposite of xenophobia, the fear of strangers, a disease many of our fellow Americans seem to have these days. Sometimes we are strangers even to ourselves, so we should show hospitality to our sometimes strange selves and then extend that same hospitality to others.

Secondly, we should be generous with the Great Narrative of Redemption. It is not ours to control or own. Jesus entrusted us with its stewardship in order that we might share it generously. It is God's unmerited gift to us. God gives this gospel to us so that we may share it with others in order that we all may abide with the One who has loved us all the way to the Cross.

Lastly, we should not only be generous with that Great Narrative, we should be flagrantly generous with it, like the sower in the parable of the sower. He did not stop to consider the worthiness of the soil. He just scattered it flagrantly and hilariously[11] and then waited for God to grow the results. In our own scattering, we should not try to impress people with our intellectual brilliance, however much we have. We should simply proclaim the gospel plainly and truthfully, and as Francis allegedly said, "Use words if we must." When such truthful proclamation occurs, Annie Dillard says the following happens: "We should all be wearing crash helmets. Ushers should issue life jackets and signal flares; they should lash us to our pews."[12]

Such is the power of God's Holy Word proclaimed. It is the Great Narrative of Redemption that will save us all. It is grace in the meantime.

NOTES

1 Aristotle, *Nicomachean Ethics*, Book 1, Section 13, trans. W. D. Ross, accessed July 6, 2016, http://classics.mit.edu/Aristotle/nicomachaen.1.i.html. Aristotle rejected the idea that happiness is a goal in and of itself. Rather it came as a result of an "activity of the soul" in pursuit of virtue.

2 *Tender Mercies*, directed by Bruce Beresford (1983; Burbank, CA: Lionsgate, 2001), DVD.

3 "Thomas Jefferson to John Page, 15 July 1763," Founders Online, National Archives, accessed July 21, 2016, http://founders.archives.gov/documents/Jefferson/01-01-02-0004.

4 The "law" here is not so much the Hebrew Law as it is a more general awareness of the indwelling sense we all have that judges us by telling us that we do not measure up; that we have failed to achieve what is expected of us. It is an exhausting pursuit of a goal we can never achieve and which then circles back on us as judgment.
5 Will Storr, "A Better Kind of Happiness," *New Yorker*, July 7, 2016, http://www.newyorker.com/tech/elements/a-better-kind-of-happiness?intcid=popular.
6 Ibid.
7 Ibid.
8 Tex told me this story in 1977 as he was mentoring me.
9 Frederick Buechner, *A Room Called Remember: Uncollected Pieces* (New York: HarperOne, 1984), 142.
10 Walter F. Miller Jr., *A Canticle for Leibowitz* (New York: Lippincott, 1959). This quote is taken from the Rule of the Order of the Ascension.
11 In 2 Corinthians 9:7, St. Paul commends all who cheerfully scatter God's abundance. The word so often translated as "cheerful" here is the Greek word *hilarion*, from which we get our English word "hilarious." It is clear to me then that "cheerful" underrepresents what St. Paul means. We are called to hilariously scatter God's abundant grace.
12 Annie Dillard, *Teaching a Stone to Talk* (New York: Harper & Row, 1982), 40.

www.ingramcontent.com/pod-product-compliance
Ingram Content Group UK Ltd.
Pitfield, Milton Keynes, MK11 3LW, UK
UKHW021841140426
5217IPUK00022B/1541